TESTIMONIALS

Tina's passion, energy, and pure optimism in life is what drives her unbelievably strong facilitation skills. Her strength in written and verbal communication is balanced with a unique ability to listen to people ... TRULY listen to people. If you as a reader truly listen, Tina will help drive your personal success while helping you be the best version of yourself each and every day.

TRUDY HARDY
VICE PRESIDENT, MARKETING, BMW OF NORTH AMERICA

Thanks for helping us to grow! To us, you are unique and majestic – like a zebra.

STUDENTS OF THE INAUGURAL
INSTRUCTOR-LED ART OF FACILITATION WORKSHOP

Tina's in the business of people. Knowing how to talk, teach, and facilitate on an individual basis with a critical sense of reading people, is her forte. She has the intellectual depth of a well-respected psychologist with the razor sharp business savvy that can go toe-to-toe with any CEO. Tina has the ability to a command a room and create an experience through speaking or through facilitating. Teaching others how to do all of these things is an art and why I hired her to run our facilitation program.

NICOLETTE STAPP CRAUMER
FORMER SENIOR MANAGER, VERIZON

As a Counselor and Facilitator of weekly groups and workshops in the addictions field, I was intrigued by this book (The ART of Facilitation). I can truly say I learned techniques that have really helped me step up my game.

I have also used some of the learnings from the book as 'life lessons' that I've taught in my Healthy Relationships Group. For example, I often use the "meeting at the restaurant" exercise on page 72, with each group member reading a different line to illustrate how inflection and tone can change the meaning of what is said. This stresses the importance of effective communication, body language and tone to my clients in a simple and engaging way.

This book should be a must read for all public speakers.

ROSE-MARY SFORZA C.A.S.A.C.-II

As a small business owner, time is of the essence and team meetings are critical; yet ours were not productive. After applying techniques learned from The ART of Facilitation, *our company's time together has become more efficient, engaging and I've seen more productivity overall. I highly recommend Tina's wise advice for any leader looking to engage their people by making just a small shift in how he/she approaches communicating. Thanks Tina!*

BRIDGETTE MCGOWAN
OWNER, BUILDERS KITCHENS

Non-profit organizations don't have time for error or delay. As the leader of the Diabetes Foundation during the Covid pandemic of 2020, our team was even more dependent on an uber high level of communication, understanding how to really listen to our participants and partners, and setting the stage for our newly-created marketing events. Tina's approach provided real-world applicable techniques on how to get engagement and even commitment from unique learning styles, how to 'set expectations' and 'over-communicate' to ensure our audience not only remembered, but participated. I highly recommend this book for anyone in sales looking to elevate their business.

GININE CILENTI
EXECUTIVE DIRECTOR, DIABETES FOUNDATION

To say that Tina is a great facilitator would be like saying Da Vinci was a so-so painter. To me, she is a MASTER. She's got the ability to connect with an audience in a way that is truly organic, transparent and REAL. What Tina has done in this book is cram almost a decade of mentoring which I received from her and put it into one easy to read and mentally digestible masterclass. Almost makes me angry. :-) If someone was looking to learn what real facilitation is all about, this book would start their journey off on the great foot, not just right foot. As a facilitator who's been in the industry for almost 2 decades, I highly recommend the teachings inside this book. Wisdom abounds!

FRANK T. ZIEDE
PROFESSIONAL FACILITATOR & OWNER
OF COMMON GROUND CONSULTING LLC

Myth busting, a facilitator's toolbox, humor and step by step guidance to becoming a presenter "they" will remember ... The ART of Facilitation has it all ... this book is easy to read and well organized. It illustrates the importance of addressing learning styles, meeting the needs of your audience, and how to use technology to enhance your presentation. The author uses hilarious examples of personal experiences to express the importance of finding and being your authentic self as a presenter. At the end of the book she includes a breakdown or quick review of the important points from each section ... A great way to help you synthesize all of the information you just read. If you are interested in becoming a facilitator or even fine tune your presentation skills, then this book is for you!

MAUREEN GORDON
GIFTED AND TALENTED TEACHER/FACILITATOR

Whether speaking to a small team or an audience of thousands, the way you communicate is the key to your message getting across successfully. In The ART of Facilitation, *Tina does a masterful job of taking the complex science of communication and facilitation and breaking it down to key factors that will take your conversation skills to the next level. Her step by step approach is easy to follow and will help even the novice presenter win over audiences. If you are looking to take the next step in your career, this book will provide you with tips and techniques that can make the ordinary, extraordinary.*

SUE NOVAK
BMW NA DEALER ENGAGEMENT &
EXPERIENCE TRAINING MANAGER

After reading Tina Clements, The ART of Facilitation, *I acquired the skills that I needed to effectively communicate with my team. Her book helped me understand the tools that I had, to help me be an effective leader and bring out the best and fullest potential of my employees and myself. Tina's knowledge and understanding of the human psyche in the workplace is priceless. I recommended this book to ANYONE in any kind of leadership role!*

STEPHANIE WALKER
PEARL RIVER FLORIST, OWNER

THE ART OF FACILITATION

Communicate So They Remember:
Bust the 15 Myths that Hold You Back!

PYP ACADEMY PRESS

Copyright © 2019, 2020 Tina Frey Clements. All rights reserved.

No part of this publication shall be reproduced, transmitted, or sold in whole or in part in any form without prior written consent of the author, except as provided by the United States of America copyright law. Any unauthorized usage of the text without express written permission of the publisher is a violation of the author's copyright and is illegal and punishable by law. All trademarks and registered trademarks appearing in this guide are the property of their respective owners.

For permission requests, write to the below address:

The Retail Performance Company, LLC (rpc)
300 Chestnut Ridge Road
Woodcliff Lake, NJ 07677

The opinions expressed by the Author are not necessarily those held by PYP Academy Press.

Ordering Information: Quantity sales and special discounts are available on quantity purchases by corporations, associations, and others. For details, contact the author at tina.clements@rpc-partners.com.

Cover design by: Cornelia Murariu
Typeset by: Medlar Publishing Solutions Pvt Ltd., India

Printed in the United States of America.

ISBN: 978-1-951591-53-3 (hardcover)
ISBN: 978-1-951591-52-6 (paperback)
ISBN: 978-1-951591-54-0 (ebook)

Library of Congress Control Number: 2020923552

Second edition, January 2021

The information contained within this book is strictly for informational purposes. The material may include information, products, or services by third parties. As such, the Author and Publisher do not assume responsibility or liability for any third-party material or opinions. The publisher is not responsible for websites (or their content) that are not owned by the publisher. Readers are advised to do their own due diligence when it comes to making decisions.

The mission of the Publish Your Purpose Academy Press is to discover and publish authors who are striving to make a difference in the world. We give underrepresented voices power and a stage to share their stories, speak their truth, and impact their communities. Do you have a book idea you would like us to consider publishing? Please visit PublishYourPurposePress.com for more information.

PYP Academy Press
141 Weston Street, #155
Hartford, CT, 06141

DEDICATION

To Ron Chatwin – The Best

TABLE OF CONTENTS

INTRODUCTION		1
STEP ONE:	The ART of Preparing	9
	Chapter 1 Understanding Learning Styles	13
	Chapter 2 The Fear Brain	27
	Chapter 3 Setting the Space – Maslow Wasn't Joking	41
	Chapter 4 Event Visuals	57
	Chapter 5 Technology: Yes?	63
STEP TWO:	The ART of the Action	69
	Chapter 6 Where Do I Put My Hands?	73
	Chapter 7 I'm Freaking Out! Why Am I So Nervous?	85
	Chapter 8 Actually Doing It	103
	Chapter 9 Handling Hecklers	123
	Chapter 10 Put a Bow on It	131
STEP THREE:	The ART of Building Your Brand	137
	Chapter 11 Establish Your ME	141
	Chapter 12 Maintain Your ME	149
CONCLUSION		155
APPENDICES		159

RECOGNITION	177
HIRE TINA TO SPEAK OR FACILITATE	179
ABOUT rpc	181
ABOUT TINA	183
BOOK CLUB QUESTIONS	185

INTRODUCTION

*The man who moves a mountain
begins by carrying away small stones.*
CONFUCIUS

During the time I was putting the final touches on this book, I facilitated a keynote address in New Orleans. The keynote was about the *Power of Choice* and I was feeling particularly confident as the topic is one I knew well and the audience was filled with relatable female entrepreneurs.

As I stepped off the stage, a young woman ran up to me and said, "I was moved by your keynote. I want to do what you do."

I smiled as I love to talk about Facilitation and it was not the first time someone had shared their feelings on the subject with me. "OK. Tell me why?" I asked. She paused thoughtfully for some time and said, "I feel like I can change lives too. And, it looks like you were having the time of your life up there."

On both points, she was right.

When you have the ability to **ARTfully** communicate your message, you can change lives; even if it's only one and even if it's only on a small scale, you can. Through this book, I would love to be the change-agent to help you on your journey to change lives and at the same time, have the time of your life.

I was a shy kid. At one point in high school, I couldn't pick up my head in the lunch room to make eye contact with students I didn't know. But, at the same time, if I knew you, I couldn't stop communicating; trying to make someone laugh, or tell a story, or add value by sharing a piece of myself. I was an enigma wrapped in a riddle.

In college, I knew I had to shift my perspective around my approach. I knew I was missing out and subconsciously, I knew I had a talent I wanted to share. I was scared, yes. But, if I didn't try to break through then, I knew I would never be able to level up; to be the person I knew I could be. So, I majored in Communication Arts and jumped into everything that scared me. I was on the college radio, took an acting class and yes, took my first presentation skills class. I started to see and feel the results of putting myself out there, trying new skills – and the consequence of my actions were fabulous. So, that was that. I might have felt shy, but I wouldn't let that feeling hold me back ever again.

During my 25+ years as a professional Communicator, I have been told "I want to do what you do" many, many times, and each time I smile knowingly, thinking about my own journey. Even though I started learning how to communicate and facilitate effectively early on in my life, it was years before I understood the real **ART** behind the science. This road is challenging, will take work and practice, but it's worth it. As they say in the movie *A League of Their Own*, if it wasn't hard, everyone would do it.

Being able to **ARTfully** communicate a message that impacts people at a high level while motivating change, is a stellar process. Whether you want to freelance facilitate and make it your life's work, facilitate within an organization, or are just want to be impactful with your message in any one-on-one situation, being a professional communicator is an inspiring and obtainable goal.

When you facilitate **ARTfully**, your world changes – you learn constantly, you get to do what you love, meet new people, stretch, grow, and you can change lives.

Facilitation is simple. Really. There are **ARTful** tools, and principles, and skills. I'll give them all to you throughout this book. Seriously, all of them.

I'll give you the myths too. As a result of the industrial age, education and learning was broken down to be rote and process driven, and many believe this is still the "correct" way to teach adults. Basically learning was delivered the same way so it could be measured en masse. This approach doesn't work, yet it's how the majority of your competition "shows up." I'll share the 15 myths that hold you back along with the myth breaking tools that help support a high level of adult learning and engagement.

To apply these tools successfully takes conscious effort, work, and practice. To be a successful and competitive Communicator, where Clients want you back time and time again, **ARTful** application is the game changer. Just being an expert on your topic du jour won't get you to the top.

To be an **ARTful** Facilitator, you also have to be ready to NOT be the center of attention (wait, what?). You have to NOT give away the farm with your answers, even if you're the absolute expert on a subject. Heck, most of the time, you never even GIVE the answer, you allow the Learner to create his/her own data and retain it. You have to practice the technique of self-control to support the **ART** of allowing the Learner to learn. In the beginning, be prepared to be wicked uncomfortable. You have to leave your ego at the door and remember that *it's all about them and not about you.* You have to believe and OWN Galileo Galilei's theory, "You cannot teach a man anything. You can only help him discover it within himself."

ARTful Facilitation is about providing knowledge and skills in a tailored, proven, mind-body experience and then getting out of the way of the Learner. That's it. You create the environment where the Learner can thrive, then step aside and allow him/her to do the work. It's like gardening, with more sweat but less dirt.

Honestly, the biggest roadblock to **ARTful** Facilitation is you.

As humans, we want to FIX. We show up and want to give all the answers. We want to take the monkey off of the back of the Participant and tame it for them. But it's not your circus and, therefore, not your monkey. The monkey needs to stay with the Participant. Translation: You can't do the work and learning for your participants. It's his or her responsibility to tame the monkey (to learn), using the skills he or she will create via your Facilitation.

Yes, when it comes to the **ART of Facilitation**, the reverse of the classic saying, "It's not you, it's me" is the objective. Hence, your first busted myth.

FACILITATION MYTH #1: IT'S ALL ABOUT ME.

It's not about you, it's about them. When **ARTfully** sharing new skills and data, the care is around the people for whom you must affect, not you. It's not about entertainment. It's not even necessarily about the data. **It's about the actual delivery of your message where the learning "sticks" with your Participants; i.e. it's retained and applied.** This will result in you being considered the best of the best in the Facilitation of your message.

While this book has an obvious heavy lilt towards actually facilitating an event or workshop, the lessons here will provide you with the skills to ultimately master the

ART of communicating your message to any audience. **As a result, Participants will learn, retain, apply, and practice at the most optimal level. They WILL remember your message.** While there is science behind Facilitation, it's knowing how to use the science to your advantage that makes it an **ARTful** experience.

Again, YOU are not doing the work for your Participants; you are the master of providing the knowledge and getting out of the way to let them "own" the experience and the materials. And here you'll receive the tools to do just that.

The more you practice these newly defined skills, the more **ARTful** you'll become to ensure the more your message is remembered. And you get to be the hero.

Let's get started.

Tina Frey Clements

Tina Frey Clements
Vice President, rpc, The Retail Performance Company
www.rpcamerica.com

STEP ONE

The ART of Preparing

WHILE IT CAN'T BE CONFIRMED as to who can take credit for the quote, the saying goes, "If I had eight hours to chop down a tree, I'd spend the first seven sharpening the saw."

The reason to prepare is to ensure your Participant feels safe and secure as they enter your "learning space." To create a successful and carefree learning environment, you must provide your Audience with the fundamental knowledge they need BEFORE the event.

This takes work and lots of energy, and perhaps other Facilitators may feel the preparation has no value. I'm here to tell you – it has ALL the value.

The prep work is the game changer. The prep work will set you apart. The prep work is what will get you invited back, or promoted, or just plain heard.

There is an **ART** to the preparation because, as they say, the devil is in the details, and the details are within your control. With that, allow me to introduce the **ART of Preparing** with a consistent focus on "controlling *everything* you can control."

CHAPTER ONE
Understanding Learning Styles

*Maybe if we tell people the brain is an app,
they'll start using it.*

ANONYMOUS

One of my mentors, Ron Chatwin said, "The brain can only absorb what the butt can endure." Ron taught me very early on that an adult has the attention span of a commercial break, must move frequently and that everyone learns in their own way. His lasting advice taught me to focus every moment while controlling what I could control.

> A FACILITATOR guides Participants through the process of learning by stimulating all learning styles, making it simple to take in data so Learners learn.

We all know the brain's capacity to learn is endless. However, so is the ability to daydream. **We have about two minutes before a Participant tunes out** and starts to think about presents they need to buy for their kid's teachers, or did I remember to shut the garage when I left the house this morning? This is normal, and regardless if you're giving a 10-minute presentation or teaching an 8-hour workshop, we Facilitators need to OWN this as our truth. We can't stop it.

Or, can we?

What keeps a Participant focused and engaged is their **desire** to be present. You can't MAKE anyone feel a certain way. However, you CAN provide information in such a way that it addresses how individual Learners take in data – and this is a game changer for you.

Enter **Learning Styles.** We all have one. To be honest, we typically have a combination of styles. As Facilitators, it's important to realize that we have the tendency to facilitate the way WE like to take in information. It's not only natural, but comfortable. However, the number one rule as a Facilitator is to remember that NOT everyone learns like you.

Because everyone learns differently and not always the way you do, every course you teach must touch on all the learning styles to ensure your group is learning effectively and staying engaged.

WHAT ARE THE LEARNING STYLES?

When you research learning styles via the inter-web, most of the results support the VARK theory. The styles are **Visual, Auditory, Reading/Writing,** and **Kinesthetic** (or Somatic). As these are the most obvious and relevant styles, we will break them down in this chapter, adding an important yet less known style called **Intellectual Learning.**

Knowing and addressing learning styles can be a real game changer within the **ART of Facilitation** and within "real life." For example, when you are communicating with your significant other, or a parent, or a child, or a friend about a topic that's important to you – how are you choosing to communicate your message? In what learning style? If the message isn't being facilitated in the way the recipient takes in information, there's a good chance the information will get lost.

> We learn with our whole self: our bodies and our minds. All parts must be actively engaged to effectively learn.

A perfect example — my pal Joe talks to me about fantasy football all the time. He talks and talks and, while I appreciate that he wants to involve me, auditory learning is not how I process and retain. So, I forget everything he just told me, almost as he's telling me. One random day we played a game of touch football with our office and during the game, he talked to me about his fantasy players and told stories about their abilities and accomplishments. This engaged my visual and kinesthetic/somatic learning style and I actually retained what was important. Let's clarify this though – the topic was important to HIM. While fantasy football is still not my thing, I retained the information he shared and was able to have a conversation at the level where Joe felt heard – and I remembered the data well into the season. Because he inadvertently attended to a portion of my personal learning style, his message was heard, understood and retained.

Lesson: Knowing your recipient's learning style not only elevates your Facilitation skills, it can essentially help you in everyday communication.

All said, the five aforementioned learning styles will be covered and broken down to provide you with comprehensive ways to communicate with your Learners. Note: We are all learning with all parts of ourselves at all times. All learning styles are relevant to all of us on some level. We learn with our whole self: our bodies and our minds. All parts must be actively engaged to effectively learn.

Learning Style One: Visual
"The Seer is Believer"

The Visual Learner is rather predominant. Most people, when asked, will say, "Oh, I'm a visual Learner. I need to see something in order to remember." It's proven that when we visualize in our mind's eye, we retain more.

Dave Meier, author of *The Accelerated Learning Handbook*, studied the effects of mental imagery on learning. On average, those who use imagery to learn technical and scientific information did 12% better on immediate recall than those who did not use imagery and 26% better on long-term retention. Even if a Participant's main learning style is not visual, studies prove that when the brain "sees," it retains.

In general, Visual Learners learn well when aided by any images, pictures, color, icons, displays, and spatial organization of elements. They also remember by creating their own images. This opens up a world of Facilitation opportunities when teaching – you can have Participants draw, work with building blocks, create with dough, develop designs, or simply close their eyes and visualize the story you're telling.

People believe their own data – using the technique of allowing Participants to "create," now you've elevated the opportunity for your Participant to retain – because the data will be their own and it's in a format that's visual and, therefore, more memorable.

Visual Learners sometimes daydream. You might think they are staring off and not paying attention when you're teaching. This could actually be true; but, most likely, they're creating, daydreaming and using the mind's eye to work out what they're learning.

Visual Learners enjoy movies. Video clips are always a great way to drive home a point visually. Use these types of complementary tools whenever appropriate, but don't overuse so as to lose the message of your material.

What works well for Visual Learners:

- Consistent images that are attached to your topics – use them frequently during your training experience to reinforce the visual. Repetition in Facilitation is welcomed and valued.

- Have Participants create their own picture based on any knowledge shared via the spoken word.

- Drawing on flipcharts. There are so many creative ways to break out your audience and have them draw. Examples could be, drawing an image of their ideal customer base or to create a process chain in a visual way, etc.

- Decorate the space. Be consistent with your branding or your Client's brand identity.

- Always have images on your presentations. During your review of the materials you have just presented, use the images as a way to remind students of your messages. Ensure any of your pre/post work and/or handouts have the same consistent images for reinforcement.

- Use room graphics – any messages you want to ensure are communicated can be turned into "wall art" and kept on hand throughout your course.

- When you can't be as visual and need to be auditory, be colorful with your verbal story; add details and "paint" a picture. Use visual, colorful, and picturesque language all the time and have the Participants close their eyes and visualize your story.

Learning Style Two: Auditory
"The Word Player"

Auditory learning goes back to the beginning of time. Before printing presses, we told stories. We gathered and learned together. There were no books, no letter carriers – it was human to human sharing of data, news of the day, oral histories, and content. That was the only way.

Auditory Learners learn best while they are actively listening. They much prefer to ingest information through audio or video clips, or by discussing a topic.

You'll know you've got yourself an Auditory Learner if you find them reading text out loud. This is an ideal way for them to retain written content because they can hear how the words sound. They may even do this dramatically – encourage this behavior when/if possible.

You may think well, this is the simplest Learner to address because all I need to do is talk and provide data, and they'll learn. While true, you must also provide ample opportunity for this Learner to interpret and talk through and ask questions around what they've heard.

What works well for Auditory Learners:

- When using computers, have Participants pair up, read to one another, and discuss.

- Ask Participants to read out loud in a classroom environment. (Be sure to ask permission and/or volunteers first before ever calling "out" a Participant. This is a Facilitation no-no.)

- Have learners paraphrase what was learned – alone or to another person.

- Have an activity where groups of Participants flipchart questions around the materials presented. Have them

ask the questions of the entire workshop group to spark dialogue from all.
- If learning a step-by-step skill, have the Auditory Learner narrate the activity while another person is doing it.

Learning Style Three: Reading/Writing
"The Book Worm"

If you're one of these types of Learners, right now, you're in heaven. No one is around, you're reading, underlining, and maybe even rewriting what you're reading. Yes, you're a Reading/Writing learner.

This Learner uses the printed word as the most important way to convey and receive information. He/she will be writing during your entire class. You might feel compelled to say, "No need to take notes, I'll be giving you all the text and PowerPoint presentation when you leave today." You'll assume this will alleviate their stress and they'll stop taking notes.

Nope.

This may actually add stress to the "Book Worm." This person has to write it down – all of it sometimes. If you are facilitating to a group, let participants know they don't need to take notes, but make a specific statement that says "but, continue onward if that's how you learn." Be sure to acknowledge your "Book Worms" when they are writing.

After writing, Reading/Writing Learners may return to their notes once they've had a chance to discuss the material in further detail. Then, they may even supplement their information with new information.

They like to see the written word and feel themselves writing. They could also turn diagrams into charts and words to help retain. This Learner makes lists and categorize their lists with headings, etc. and are a fan of handouts, textbooks, and appreciate lots of context in sentences.

Some Learners will make their own glossary of words, read them over, and then create a new, condensed set of study notes. They are a fan of rewriting explanations and notes out into their own words. They know, if they can't rewrite a definition or describe a concept in their own words, concisely, there is a good chance that there is an aspect of that concept that they don't fully understand. So, they need to read again.

What works well for Reading/Writing Learners:

- Provide handouts with blanks and encourage Participants to fill in the blanks throughout the class.
- Break into groups of two and share notes on what was learned. Provide time for rewriting of notes.
- Provide plenty of note paper to encourage this Learner to support their natural learning style.
- Use bullet pointed listed to allow this Learner to interpret the learning and rewrite it on their own.
- Create an activity where a diagram is broken down into words.

Learning Style Four: Kinesthetic or Somatic
"The Mover"

The word Somatic comes from the Greek word for body.

This style has long been at a disadvantage in our western culture and style of learning. Do you remember the old song, "reading and writing arithmetic, sung to the tune of a hickory stick?"

The song reminds us of the "factory" model mentality and that children were physically punished for not confirming to the norm of being taught and tested the exact same way. Think about that. It's been embedded in so many of us that, as teachers, we cannot allow children to get up and move; to do what comes naturally to them. Educators in a different era had it backwards, they just didn't know it.

For Somatic Learners, by not allowing them to engage with their bodies, we're compromising their minds to be used at their full potential. As a Facilitator, you need to be okay if someone is playing with clay or dough while you're talking, or getting up and walking around, or doodling like crazy. They're engaged, in their own way.

You learn well when you can move your body and/or use your hands and engage your sense of touch. Writing or drawing diagrams or doodling are physical activities that can definitely fall into this category.

"The Mover" likes to move around, touch, and talk. They express with body language, interact with space, and process knowledge through body sensations.

What works well for Kinesthetic/Somatic Learners:

- If you're teaching about a process, use people to "become" part of a process. Create a breakout activity where the Participants become the "widget" or the "piece of the factory" process, and physically move and use the room.

- Always, always have kinesthetic/somatic devices on the table. Play dough, stress balls, pipe cleaners, etc. During a lecture or when it's necessary to be talking to your group, this Learner can grab a piece of play dough and crush it to his/her heart's content. It keeps their body engaged and, therefore, the mind.

- Flipchart anything. Having Participants stand up and write is simple and an elegant way to engage.

- Scavenger hunts. This takes prep and it's a great way to learn and be very active.

- When you don't have the latitude to allow Learners to break out or be active, ask safe rhetorical questions of the group that add value to what you're sharing. Then, raise your own hand indicating to your group that you want them to raise their hands in return. This engages people physically without hijacking your lecture. It keeps people active and they don't even know it.

Learning Style Five: Intellectual
"The Sense Maker"

Don't you dare get to H before you teach A through G. This type of Learner needs to learn in order. He/she is a processor of information and is internally reflecting and understanding new data in the order in which it comes.

The "Sense Maker" is exactly that, trying to make sense of the data so he/she can move onto the next piece of data. They are linear thinkers who reflect to create connections and meaning within the learning. If they have not sufficiently created their own plan/pathway around the new data, or if they haven't had the chance to problem-solve or even integrate the data in their own minds, they will be stuck.

This style can be crippling to Learners where the Facilitator has no clue of this style and teaches "all over the place" with no order. As this is my primary learning style, I once had to leave a four-day course on the second day because the content from the first day was so unorganized. I felt so behind because I was unable to sort all the information out in time to learn the data efficiently, and I checked out.

This can be a challenge for a Facilitator because, well, there is usually a schedule. We have commitments to our Clients and other Participants to keep the flow going, yet we do need to ensure the Intellectual Learners are still with us as we progress.

Therefore you must ensure the data you're teaching is provided in such a way that it's linear in nature and that there's time to work through the understanding. If you're a Kinesthetic/Somatic Facilitator, this can be a challenge as you may feel constricted. Teaching in order does not mean you can't off script and detour to follow the needs of the Participants – you certainly can and should if the class dictates the need. However, you must at some point get the learning back on track and ensure the linearity of the learning is intact.

What works well for the Intellectual Learner:

- Be sure your content is taught "in order."
- Provide time for the group to talk about a topic that was just presented. Or, give table teams a problem to solve based on the topic.
- Provide time for personal reflection after a module; with writing or just time to themselves. Then ask the group to share feedback, questions, or general revelations.
- Create an activity where teams must use the new knowledge and apply it directly to a situation in their worlds. Real world, real time.

In Summary:

Along our journey, humans adopted a factory style of learning where we printed words and taught the exact same way expecting a consistent result.

There's absolute proof that learning takes on all shapes and styles because no human lives in a box. Not a behavioral box, a strength-based box, and certainly not a learning box. We take in and retain information in a plethora of ways.

Be sure to keep your Participants mind and body connected and physically engaged. Set them up for success to retain by touching on ALL learning styles, not just your own.

FACILITATION MYTH #2:
EVERYONE LEARNS THE SAME WAY.

CHAPTER TWO
The Fear Brain

Courage is fear holding on a minute longer.
GEORGE S. PATTON

The brain is a funny, funny thing. And, it's old; set in its ways.

When humans were cavemen, we were rooted in simplicity. We needed to survive. To do so, we needed to protect ourselves, be secure, and ease tension.

This brain function has not changed and believe it or not, has a very big part in the creation of a successful training event. How? In two specific ways:

- Participant's fear prior to the course
- Participant's fear during the course

Fear is probably the most researched and, hopefully, best understood of all the emotions. It's the easiest to study because it has the most measurable physiological response and it's also the most important emotion we have from an evolutionary standpoint.

> Your fear-based 'noise' saves you the PAIN OF FAILING.

Learning to fear something dangerous that caused pain in the past, like a charging saber tooth tiger, (or more recently, like a spider), most likely helped us as a species to survive. Now evolution has taken that primal fear and used it to bypass danger that comes in the form of the 'noise' in our own minds as opposed to a ginormous *T. rex* that might attack us on our way to the grocery store. (Or, again, a spider.)

Like I said, the brain is a funny thing. And, if scary dinosaurs no longer exist, what is the 'noise' of which I speak?

The 'noise' can go deep and, quite frankly, fear-based 'noise' is what humans create in their own minds to keep them small; to keep them safe from the pain of failure. This fear can be as simple as the fear of being late – but, really the 'noise' is saying, "I'm very shy and if I'm late the teacher may call me out when I enter the room and I can't bear the thought of being embarrassed like that."

Are you thinking, "Really – how deep are we going to get here? I thought this book was about getting others to retain my message."

While I won't get too deep, I promise, it's critical to understand enough of the WHY humans behave to help you engage in some of the WHAT.

Some fun facts as to why the fear even happens:

- Fear starts in the region of the brain called the amygdala.
- The amygdala's job is to detect fear, the importance of the stimuli, and then prepare for the emergency event.
- The fear spreads through the body to make adjustments for the best defense – enter, the "fight or flight" reaction.

Here's what's interesting – The amygdala is the reason we are afraid of things outside our control. We produce a biological and chemical response that prepares us to be efficient in danger. The brain becomes hyper alert and pupils actually dilate, breathing accelerates, blood pressure rises, and processes not considered vital in survival like digestion slow down.

Now, the good news is, we can control a lot of your student's potential fear with some simple techniques. If we can proactively understand the brain and use the knowledge to our advantage to CONTROL EVERYTHING WE CAN CONTROL, then as a result, your Participants will *FEEL* AS IF THEY'RE IN CONTROL.

As a result of controlling everything you can control, you'll have a superior advantage over your competition and ultimately enjoy your experience because of all of your prework. Just because you managed the brain's reptilian fear.

Not to oversimplify, here's what we can totally control – EXPECTATION SETTING.

> Setting your Participants' expectations is a total GAME CHANGER.

If I've said this once, I've said it 10,458 times, setting your Participants' expectations is a total game changer. You can CONTROL this and it's so simple. While it does take work, time and energy, it pays off in the end big time. Expectation setting includes all of the communication you'll control via the techniques I'll share now.

While simple, you'd be surprised how few organizations or Facilitators apply these techniques. Perhaps because they are simple they're overlooked; yet they're so important and critical to success.

What techniques can we apply to help Participants feel in control and be devoid of tension days/weeks prior to an event and on the day they arrive?

Glad you asked …

TECHNIQUES TO CONTROL WHAT YOU CAN CONTROL

ONE: *Pre-work*

Pre-work is a very important part of a training event. Many Facilitators don't engage because it takes a bit of effort. Pre-work can be as simple as asking Participants to read a book, answer a quiz, or be requested to send an email regarding their list of objectives for the class. Whatever method is appropriate to get the Participants engaged and focused around the topic at hand before the event will do the trick.

Now, you may actually need to have Participants do real work prior to the event. For example, if the course you're teaching is around how to diagnose an engine failure, you may want to have your Participants read a document with specific components and where they're located in the vehicle. This gives you and the Participants the ability to ensure the class is on the same page upon entrance and it's a time saver.

Regardless of the level of pre-work, this act starts the process of a tension reduction for the student because it acclimates them to your topic and what will be taught live.

TWO: *When in Doubt,* OVER COMMUNICATE

As soon as your students register, they should receive a bounty of information regarding your course via email. This should come immediately and consistently. As an added value, send something in the mail. (Yes, the actual mail.) This can include a hand-written card, detailed directions on how to get to the event, logistic information or even a coffee gift card as a special touch.

Emails, phone calls, and general communication should continue up until the day before your event. Do your best with your communication to answer every single question a Participant may have.

These constant communications will help with 95% of your audience and make your life much easier in the long run. Those that don't read the emails until the day before the event (or even the morning of) will still find at least one of the notes you've sent and get the data they need to be successful. Those that need a little more handholding and who did read the notes will feel very secure as they've felt a high level of communication from the beginning. All because you controlled what you could control.

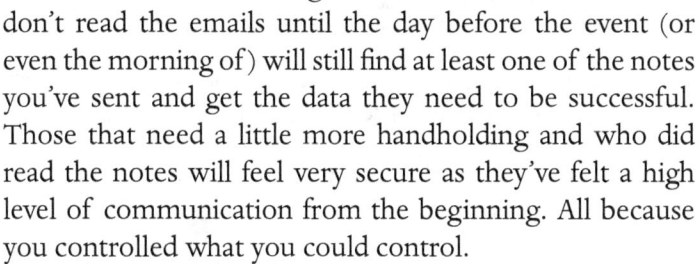

Here's what I recommend regarding pre-work communication:

1) Once Participants register, they should receive an immediate email with an enthusiastic confirmation of registration.

2) Within one day of registering, an email from you, or the company for which you are working, should go to the Participant with details on what to expect from the class. It should include the following:

- What to wear
- Start/end times
- How to check in, if necessary
- What to bring – license, any specific documents, laptops, etc.
- Any cancellation information (e.g., up until what point can they cancel, any cancellation fees, etc.)
- What is financially covered. (e.g., is the cost of travel the responsibility of the Participant, or is some of it covered by the class sponsor?)
- If they will be fed
  - if they will, provide a way to communicate dietary restrictions with ease
- Where the event will take place in excruciating detail
  - are you in a specific suite inside a specific building?
  - if it's a challenge to park, tell them to come early and explain why it's a challenge if needed
  - is parking paid for if the event is in a city and parking in a lot is necessary
  - if you're in a hotel, is there valet; do you reimburse for valet
  - if the building is generally hard to find as it's hidden; ex. in a mall, in a plaza
  - if a navigation system in a vehicle cannot securely get them to your class, communicate this and provide a close alternative with instructions on how to find the location
  - if the location is in a high traffic area, communicate this so they will allot extra travel time

Once you've sent this logistic note, you'll send it again and again. Be prepared as some folks will be late or lost even with all of your efforts.

> SEE APPENDIX (pp. 161–162) for templates of pre-work handouts.

3) Consistently communicate. Send an email a week up until the event. The goal of these emails is to maintain excitement for the event and to remind the Participants of their commitment. You'd be surprised how people enthusiastically register for an event and then completely forget about it until the night before.

The email should be short and impactful. Remind them of the event and give them a "tidbit" about what they'll learn. Perhaps share a quote, or recommend a book, or a have a link to a video or even a short exercise. Something that is relevant to the class and brings value in a very short paragraph.

Again, resend the logistic details in an attached word document. Attach this within every email. Don't spell it out in detail within the note because your email will look monstrous and no one will engage to read it.

4) Call. If you're able to pick up a phone and call the Participant within a few days of the event, you will be rocked by the positive outcome. This will drive confidence, engagement, and assurance that you will meet their expectations during the class. This will also reduce the "no-show" effect by a million percent. By hearing your voice and verbally committing to you, a Participant becomes subconsciously accountable and you've made it very hard for him/her to "blow you off."

I'll give you a simple personal example of why all of this

aforementioned info and these techniques are critical. I was meeting a new doctor in NJ, and the number of the address had a dash in it, something like 5-12 Main Street (I knew right away I was in trouble). When I made the appointment, the receptionist did not give me any special instructions nor was there any detailed email sent prior to my appointment.

Via my navigation system (one of man's truly best inventions after the paper towel), I arrived at 5-12 Main Street, which was actually a nail salon. Excellent. I found my way into a shopping plaza and zipped around for an extra 15 minutes to finally find the office off of Main Street, on a side avenue. I arrived stressed, sweating, angry at anyone at the front desk who had ears, and all I wanted to do was not be there.

Have I painted a picture? This is real. Emotion like this can seriously affect your Participant's experience negatively. Can you avoid this for your folks with some simple emails, expectations setting, and a phone call? Yes. Yes you can.

I understand this takes a lot of time and energy and I'm also clear of the value it brings. Do it.

THREE: *Start Your Face-to-Face Communication with CLEARLY Defined Expectations*

We can debate if you want to open up any communication event with an immediate activity or with verbal expectation setting – I have done both and both have a purpose.

Most of the time however, I recommend that as your Students are taking their seats and getting their last cup of coffee, you want to have set their expectations set and know what to expect from their day within minutes.

Expectation setting is the act of showing respect to your Participants by telling them what to expect in terms of their 1) hierarchal needs/logistics, 2) who you are, and 3) the class objectives. That's really all there is to it.

What needs to be communicated immediately?

1) The name of the class and what it is. Yes, every once in a blue moon, you get a Participant who shouldn't be in the room. Seriously. It happens. But really, we do this to frame the introduction and, in general, "get started."

Next, share details around when lunch will be served, where to find more coffee, where the bathrooms are located, what time the day will end, and so on. These details are so subtle and so many communicators overlook the necessity of sharing. By taking a minute to address those hierarchical needs, Participants will feel more relaxed and open to learning.

2) Next, who are you? Yes, we've told you that **ARTful Facilitation** is NOT about you; however, you're there. You're standing in the front of the room and everyone would like to know what gives you the right to be there. So, tell them – swiftly.

I like to use a PowerPoint to share where I've worked and my history within the Learning and Development

(L&D) field. The goal is to build credibility and do so in a visual way.

If you have experience within the content you're facilitating (i.e. if you're Facilitating how to skydive and you've been a skydiver for 20 years), share this as well. Yes it's important that there is credibility around your ability to facilitate. However, if you also have credibility and know-how within the topic du jour, by all means, share.

Can you share personal images and stories? Yes, but within reason. It's good to remind Participants that you're human, but it's not good to distract from the reason YOU have been chosen to facilitate. I experienced a Facilitator who spent 10 minutes on his personal life and he actually lost credibility because he set expectations that his presence in the class was not the most important thing in his life. At that moment, all of his Participants wanted US to be the most important thing. So, yes, share who you are but do it in a way that supports you as a Facilitator.

3) Next, define the "why." Why are the Participants there: what is the course about, what will they take away, and why is all of it important to them. This can be done quickly or, depending on the need, this can be a series of questions and even an activity.

An objective slide is very helpful and a general rule is to not have more than 3 objectives for an event. If so, the class would typically be more than one day. A human can't be expected to take away more than three objectives. (Again, all is contingent on many factors like length of class, need, Client goals, etc.)

At this point, it's also ideal to learn and share the Participant's desires for the class. Either this information can come to you via the pre-work requested or, we stop here and ask for feedback from the class and flipchart the answers. The latter is old-school, but works well; which is why we still do it.

Note: If you ask for the Participant's course objectives, you absolutely must revisit them throughout the class and especially at the end of the event. Humans need acknowledgment and closure and, by not attending to their objectives, you're effectively providing a new tension. Remember, control what you can control.

In Summary:

"Failure is a direct result of poorly set expectations." –*Said by someone famous at some famous point in time.*

A big key to you facilitating **ARTfully** is to control as many variables as possible. By setting expectations within your control, you've done just that.

Really think about all of the brain conversation we've had; how we take things in and how we process and think and feel. All of this emotion, reaction, explosion of energy is happening possibly by a Participant NOT having clear direction on where to park their car.

It doesn't matter what the "what" is. The point is, we know that our little cavemen brains are hard-wired to react to fear. And, for many, a training class can evoke fear.

So, under the title of, "control what you can control," what can we control and help ease tension prior to an event and at the start of an event?

A lot.

Do everything possible to prepare your students for everything. Your goal is to allow the feeling of control and ease tension to allow a Participant (and his/her brain) to be open to the data you're sharing. It benefits you GREATLY if the Participant is at ease. If he/she is not nervous, or worried about something as silly as what time is lunch, your chance of overall success increases tenfold.

FACILITATION MYTH #3:
YOU HAVE NO CONTROL OVER YOUR PARTICIPANTS' FEELINGS.

CHAPTER THREE

Setting the Space – Maslow Wasn't Joking

The two things in life you are in total control over are your attitude and your effort.

BILLY COX

What's the big deal? We need chairs and a table and we're good to go. Right?

Oh my ... it actually hurts my soul to write that, even writing it sarcastically.

This topic really should be housed with the pages supporting the brain because walking into a environment that has been ideally and **ARTfully** set, is another game changer. It's so important, I gave it its own chapter.

When you have properly set a space, you provide tension reductions. Tension comes from fear and well, you know the rest from chapter two.

So, how do we continue to control what we can control, have the Participant feel in control, and produce a tension reduction? These ideas are quite basic and they stem from Maslow's Hierarchy of Needs.

Abraham Maslow is the 10th most cited psychologist of the 20th century. He created his hierarchy of needs in 1943 and it's still relevant today. His approach was to focus on self-actualization and growth versus treating people like "a bag of symptoms." This gave him insight into how people react under a wide range of conditions. He's also known for Maslow's Hammer, the saying that "If all you have is a hammer, everything looks like a nail." (One of my most favorite quotes of all times.)

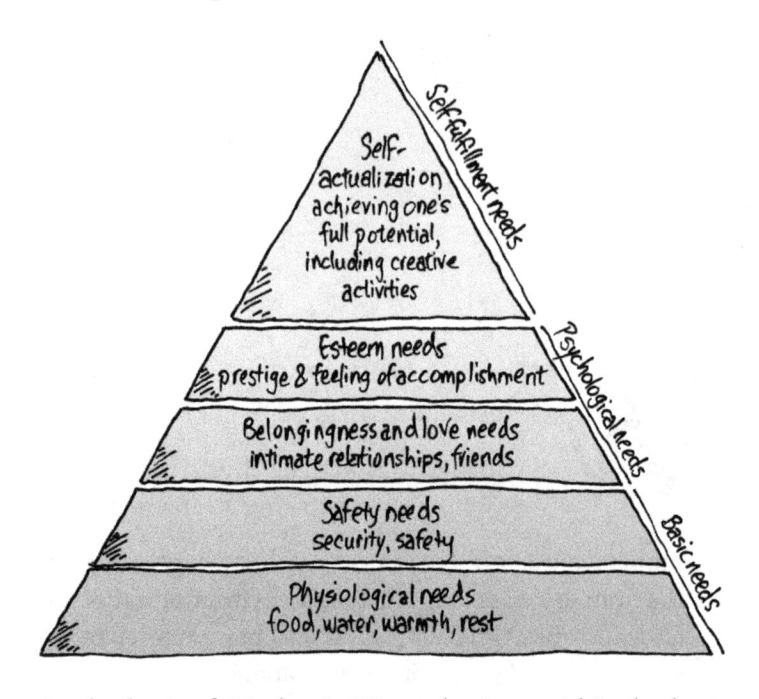

Pyramid diagram of Maslow's Hierarchy of Needs:
- Self-actualization: achieving one's full potential, including creative activities (Self-fulfillment needs)
- Esteem needs: prestige & feeling of accomplishment (Psychological needs)
- Belongingness and love needs: intimate relationships, friends
- Safety needs: security, safety (Basic needs)
- Physiological needs: food, water, warmth, rest

At the base of Maslow's Hierarchy Pyramid is the basic physiological needs for survival: food, water, warmth, and rest. As you go up the pyramid, the needs change from basic to psychological to self-fulfillment. You can't get to the top, however, unless all of the needs below are fulfilled. For our purposes, the higher up on the pyramid you are, the easier it is to learn. If the needs at the bottom aren't met – if you're hungry, tired, or uncomfortable – it's going to be very difficult to learn. Good Facilitators are aware of their Participants and work to eliminate tensions that prevent learning.

As Facilitators, we're responsible for Participants' learning and that starts with creating a safe, comfortable environment. Yes, we can control this. Environment, group dynamics, fostering belonging and esteem, etc. – all controllable.

As we know, the more you reduce tension on your Learners, the better their ability to take on new information, and, as we've already learned, stress activates the wrong reaction. Let's not confuse memory with learning. A stressful event can be memorable, but people don't learn when stressed out. In fact, some studies have shown that stressed adults do up to 50% worse in cognitive tests than low stress adults (Brain Rules, John Medina).

As a Facilitator, stress is the enemy. Our approach to "control what you can control" comes directly from Maslow's Hierarchy as you can control almost everything within his pyramid. When we focus on the pyramid, the ability to reduce or remove tension from your Participants is simple, yet masterful.

ONE: *Signage*

After you've done a tremendous job of over-communicating and your Participants have shown up to your training venue (on time), they still need to find the actual event space.

Sounds simple to control right? It's so simple, yet the act of physically guiding Participants to their learning location is typically overlooked.

Signage should be supportive of the Corporate Identity (CI) of the organization for whom your working, and/or on the topic you're communicating. Signage should be everywhere, especially if finding the location is complicated. If you can't support CI and can't finance the creation of graphic elements, then still make the effort to hand write signage or, ask the facility with whom you're working to help you. Do what you need to do to make signage happen – it's very important.

As an example, if your event is held within your massive organizational building and folks are new to the facility, don't leave them to find their way on their own. Have greeters and place signs that mirror your CI wherever possible. Don't leave it to chance that your people will know where to go, that they can "figure it out" on their own, or that they'll have the nerve to ask someone. Don't set your Participants up to fail when you can set them up for success. Take out the guess work and create your own form of breadcrumbs to get them where they need to be as easily as possible.

Has an airline ever lost your luggage and you needed to find the lost bag counter to start the process to retrieve them? Anyone who has experienced this knows it's a stressful situation. What makes it even more stressful is how challenging it is to find the lost bag counter! It can be daunting and overwhelming to find your way in any new experience, especially when you're already feeling nervous. Attending a live experience for the first time is no different. Keep this I mind and ensure your folks are guided to your experience stress free with the use of just a few signs and a little of your time.

TWO: *Music*

"Music gives a soul to the universe, wings to the mind, flight to the imagination and life to everything." *–Plato*

The use of music is yet another game changer and can (and should) be used as your Participants enter your event, leave your event, during breaks and appropriate activities.

Music is important as it's an immediate tension breaker, for the mere fact that the room is not silent. Have you ever walked into a room full of people and it's so quiet, you feel intimidated enough to not want to say good morning?

A lot of the tension can live within the energy it takes to just put your foot into a room and have to meet new people. It can be super hard and scary for some Participants, and music is like a warm blanket on a rainy day.

As your Participants draw close to your training room (which they'll find easily because of all the signs), they should hear uplifting music providing them with their first sense of ease and comfort.

As a general rule, "entrance" music is higher energy and should be loud enough for everyone to hear, but not too loud that they can't speak over it to chat and bond. Also, your music has to be censored. No cursing or abusive language of any kind. Remember, it's not about you ever – it's about the Participants and the music should be generic enough to be appreciated by all.

Some examples of good entrance/upbeat music:

- Happy – Pharrell Williams
- Don't Stop Believing – Journey
- Ain't No Mountain High Enough – Marvin Gaye & Tammi Terrell
- September – Earth Wind & Fire
- Bye Bye Bye – *NSYNC
- Ray of Light – Madonna
- Chicago – Sufjian Stevens
- Walking on Sunshine – Katrina & the Waves
- Can't Stop the Feeling – Justin Timberlake
- ABC – The Jackson Five
- Wake Me Up – Avicii
- Shake it Off – Taylor Swift

- Good Feeling – Flo Rida
- Signed Sealed Delivered (I'm Yours) – Stevie Wonder
- Get Lucky – Daft Punk
- 1901 – Phoenix
- Applause – Lady Gaga
- Cecilia – Simon & Garfunkle
- Freedom 90 – George Michael
- My Girl – The Temptations
- Something Just Like This – The Chainsmokers
- There She Goes – The La's
- Groove is in the Heart – Deee-Lite
- Stuck in the Middle with You – Stealers Wheel
- Best Day of My Life – American Authors
- I Want You Back – The Jackson 5
- Better Together – Jack Johnson
- December, 1963 (Oh What a Night) – Frankie Vali & The Four Seasons

When it's time for an activity and you're asking for groups to work together, music is a perfect buffer. It once again provides a tension reduction as there won't be any silence while Participants enter into their conversations. The ideal music for activities has no words. The music can have energy, but should be there to be behind the scenes, supporting and not distracting. This is the wrong time for Vanilla Ice or C&C Music Factory.

Some examples of "chilled out" music you'd use during activities:

- Clouds – IHF
- Albany – Kev Brown
- Saint Germain – DJ Cam Quartet

- Soundgirl Personal – Fat Jon
- Cia – Karriem Riggins
- Grass – baaskaT
- Early Morning Chill – Yams
- Sour Soul – BADBADNOTGOOD
- Smooth While Raw – Gramatik
- Depths – Guustavv
- Lampin' – ocean jams
- Crystal Ship – soder
- I'd Rather Sleep – Smartface
- Not over Yet – GentleBeatz
- Spruce – bitbeats
- Lakeview – Karuna
- Golfi – Mora
- Brunch – jobii
- Bae Bae – Kid Taro
- Sweet Berries – Handbook
- When the Time Comes – Gordon
- Coliseium – omniboi
- Ooohwee – Monma
- Pitter Patter – Guustavv

Exit music, same as entrance. Upbeat, appropriate, and should be turned on as soon as the Participants are applauding you after they participate in the the best experience in the whole wide world.

NOTE: If you're able to conduct a survey of your Participants prior to your experience, ask them their favorite songs. You can then create a play-list of entrance and exit music with their favorite tunes of all time. Talk about personalizing an experience. (Remember to censor however!)

THREE: *Table Arrangements*

Ideally, when you're facilitating a course, you have at least 12 Participants and the course is interactive. That's ideal.

We are not always so lucky to have the ideal situation and we need to make due. When we have the control, you want a room that has table rounds with no more than six people at a table. This set up immediately supports teamwork, comradery and an easy platform for Participants to work together. It also creates an ideal space for you, the **ARTful Facilitator**, to move about the cabin and work the room.

Now, this the ideal set-up scenario. Sometime, we need to work with what we have.

If you have no tables, then create a U set up or a group of Us. Again, this creates a space where interaction and support are psychologically now engrained and expected. At times, a U set up is even better than rounds – typically when you're facilitating emotional intense activities. i.e. if you're working a group though conflict or teaching a course around trust. This type of set up is ideal to "force" the closeness by removing the literal boundaries between people.

Conference rooms. Not my favorite. They're awkward, don't promote interactivity and it's a challenge to move and facilitate activities. Still, as an **ARTful Facilitator**, you can successfully communicate in this space as long as you're prepared and have created activities knowing your situation up front.

I threw a wedding-shower for 20 people in a conference room once and facilitated a typical wedding-shower game prior to the event. I had everyone back away from the table and create groups of 3 to play "Name the Spice." Because I had set everyone's expectations on the space prior to the event, and created an activity where a table wasn't necessary, the event went very well. Again, not ideal, but when you control what you can control, you can **ARTfully Facilitate** anywhere, even during a fire drill in a hotel conference room if necessary. (Yes, I did that once too.)

FOUR: *What's All That Stuff on the Tables?*

Let's get back to the Kinesthetic/Somatic Leaner we discussed earlier. Statistically, humans retain longer and more if they're using their entire brain/body connection.

Well, here's where all these crazy items on the tables come into play.

During any Facilitation sometimes, you have to talk. You'll have to run through some data and/or some instructions and people will just have to listen. To help with retention and attention, kinesthetic/somatic devices are important; nay, critical.

What's unreal to me is how many courses or even meetings I've attended over the years that never any devices on the table. Adding devices will elevate your game immediately and they are easy to source. For example, a great resource is Trainers Warehouse. *www.trainerswarehouse.com.*

Under the title "kinesthetic/somatic learning tools" is a plethora of items ideal for your needs like:

- Koosh balls
- Fiddle blocks
- Puddy
- Pipe Cleaners
- Olfactory (nice smelling) markers

As an added value, create tent cards with your Participants names and put them on the table prior to their entry. Tension reductions float out of a person who sees their own name because they're assured they have "arrived" to where they're supposed to be and honestly, they just feel special. Tent cards are easy to print or, as a way to ensure you remember names, hand write them yourself. The act of writing will help you remember.

FIVE: *Scent*

Yes. Smells.

Of all your senses, memory has the strongest link to your olfactory. Yes, your schnozz.

Using scent in your experience, classroom, or even on your person is a great way to create an ideal environment, affect mood, and memory.

I have never experienced a presentation, a class or an event outside of our own where the scent was a controlled and conscious choice. It's just not a focus for most Facilitators. The mere act of attaching a scent to your experience will elevate your game and create a competitive environment. So, why not consider it?

Really, we do it to continue to create a comfortable environment to spark learning. When the Learners leave and they smell the familiar smell in the future, they'll be brought back to their feelings when they were with YOU – to your experience, to what they learned, and they will remember.

So how? How does this work?

Our noses have at least 1,000 smell receptors which receive a ton of data. When we smell, our body processes the odor with the olfactory bulb starting in the nose and running along the bottom of the brain. It has direct connections to two brain areas that are strongly implicated in both emotion and memory: the hippocampus; a nerve responsible for associative learning (which is the process by which one event or item comes to be linked to another because of an individual's past experiences) and the amygdala (which we've learned about earlier), which is responsible for processing emotion. So, when you first smell something, our brain immediately links its scent to a moment, event, or person. Voila!

Interestingly, visual, auditory (sound), and tactile (touch) information do not pass through these brain areas and it's suggested that this is a part of the reason why smelling is so successful at triggering emotions and memories.

When you smell things you remember your emotions. Fact. Knowing this, you have the power to attach a scent to you and your brand. The scent should be subtle, yet memorable and of course, likeable.

Some popular and subtle scents include:

- Blue Spruce
- Cinnamon
- Clean Cotton
- Lavender
- Apple
- Vanilla

Very critical point. The scent cannot offend, nor be too strong. I have had a few bad experiences where students literally became nauseous at the smell of a "clean linen" incense burner. It was not pretty. Test your scent, be sure it's not too much for your space, and creates the long lasting memory you're looking for. Keep it subtle and non-offensive.

When adding scent, safety first. A diffuser or oil burner using a light bulb is a personal choice as it's safe and the scent is usually not overwhelming. There are wall plug-ins that use oil and are very convenient however, be aware that the scent could overpower and have an adverse effect. Candles are a great choice however I never recommend. Unless you're facilitating outside on how to make s'mores, I would stay away from fire altogether.

SIX: *Food and Beverage*

Coffee. Have it.

In all seriousness, keeping your Participants fed and hydrated is a basic need you can control. Whenever possible, have food and beverages on hand in your training space. This will not only ensure your Participants are satiated, it also dissuades them from the act of wandering off.

If you're able to control your food and beverage options for your experience, consider the following:

- Dietary restrictions. During your pre-work, you would have asked this question and can support any specific needs with ease. There is always a good chance at least one of your Participants has some sort of allergy or a special need; to be able to control it up front is ideal.

- Have vegetarian options.

- Have fruit options along with desert options.

- Provide foods that are least likely to make people drowsy. Who doesn't love Thanksgiving dinner? However, having heavier items such as turkey and Mom-like-homemade-stuffing might not be ideal. Foods like salad options, vegetables and lemon chicken will better support your Learner's ability to keep their head in the game.

- If you're facilitating for an entire day, stay ahead of the snacks. Be sure your space has ample nourishment and if your event is catered, have the afternoon snacks brought it directly following lunch to ensure they're on hand. This will help to have less interruptions in the afternoon and ensure your people have what they need.

If you are only able to provide the absolutely basics, shoot for the following must-haves:

- Water
- Coffee/Tea
- Sodas
- Portable foods – granola bars, bags of chips, apples, bananas

For some of us, our Client is responsible to manage and finance this controllable piece of your **ARTful** experience. This means, your event may not be supported with any food or beverages. While I have been lucky enough to work with Clients who understand the critical nature of having the basic provisions, there are certainly Clients who are unable to support. When this happens, start your training by communicating to your Participants the details on where to find nourishment. Ensure them you

> Focus on your Participant's basic needs; REDUCE THEIR TENSION with constant breaks and nourishment.

will provide adequate breaks to allow the opportunity to get what they need to sustain themselves through the day. At the very least, this will provide the tension reduction needed to get maintain their focus and engagement.

People need nourishment and more importantly, need to know when they'll be breaking to have it. Plan accordingly and control what you can control.

SEVEN: *Start and Set Up Your Course with CLEARLY Defined Expectations*

We already spoke to this when discussing "over communication." To reiterate, always be sure to start the class right off the bat with the following information:

- The location of the bathrooms
- Name of class and objective of the experience
- About you. Who are YOU anyway?
- How/when to use their phones/make calls
- When they'll eat lunch and get snacks
- What time the class is over

Give them comfort by answering the questions bringing them tension. Then they're left feeling confident and their brains are fully open for whatever gifts you're about to give them.

In Summary:

The Devil is in the details. Control what you can control in regard to your space and you'll see a continued tension reduction and even a few smiles throughout your experience.

FACILITATION MYTH #4: THAT'S NOT MY JOB.

CHAPTER FOUR
Event Visuals

Design is intelligence made visible.
ALINA WHEELER

F or this chapter, we focus on the use of PowerPoint (PPT) and room peripherals.

Why are they important?

- They encourage learning by supporting specific adult learning styles.
- They set the stage for the topics and concepts you will cover.
- They create a unique environment that's different from Participants' typical offices or boardrooms; one where a Participant can become immersed in your learning.
- They become key tools for you to reinforce important themes and take-aways throughout your experience.
- They're the ideal "cheat sheet" for a Facilitator, and no one has to know but you.

> Visuals serve as a TRANSITION FROM THE OUTSIDE world into your consciously-created learning environment.

Visuals in the room help to serve as a transition from the outside world to your meeting space. This is an important component to continue to reduce tension on the Learner. Outside your room, your Participants have busy lives with bosses, meetings, emails, and deadlines. Inside your room, you need them to focus on you and your message. You can use visuals to help your Participants transition out of their normal lives and into your learning environment.

Regarding slide presentations, there are some simple, yet important guidelines to keep in mind when creating them:

- Remember the goal is to NOT have all the information your Learner needs on a slide. The point is to have short, bulleted info that reflects the topics at hand. YOUR job is to deliver the data – the PPT is just a compliment to YOU.

- The fewer words the better. Prioritize images.

- Try to keep it to no more than five bullet points per slide and six words per bullet. A PPT is not meant to be read by the audience. It's there for a reference only!

- Use big fonts so people at the back of the room can read the slides.

- Use common, easy-to-read fonts. Arial is a great choice. Comic Sans is not.

- Keep content out of the corners of the slide.

- Be consistent with your slides. Do NOT use different fonts for each bullet or each page. Consistency is key.

- Use graphics, but don't get cocky. You are the person delivering the messages; don't lean on the PPT to be entertaining. It will be too distracting.

- If creating the PPT for a client, be sure to follow their Corporate Identity (CI) rules to a T.

- Embed any videos or audio possible. This creates a clean, professional show (making your life easier) and adds a touch of polish to your presentation.

The truth is, the PPT's main purpose is this – it's YOUR cheat sheet. (Don't tell.)

Yes, the PPT is great for the visual learner and to help with retainment of your message for your audience. And the more visuals, the better. However, an important reason the PPT exists is to ensure you are on track and are staying organized to cover all of the most important points of your objectives.

Be sure while using your slides as a cheat sheet, you're not reading from them or married to them. Translation: your audience knows how to read. Don't do that for them; they'll do it faster than you anyway. However, never put anything on the slides and expect it to be ignored. If it's there, expect it to be read and you ignored. This is another reason we keep the data on the slides short; more visuals and less words whenever possible.

> SEE APPENDIX (p. 169) for a PowerPoint checklist.

A fun fact here is to use the function on your clicker or laptop to white out the screen if you've realized your audience is engaging in the **ART** of reading, when you need them to be focusing on your presentation. (Most clickers or laptops have this functionality.)

At times, you'll come across a slide for which you have no interest in supporting or maybe you left in your deck by mistake. This is where you can do one of two things. 1) blast past the slide and keep going or 2) use your improv technique to acknowledge the moment. You'll learn more in chapter eight around improv, however really all I mean here is you acknowledge that you saw the slide, and that you're consciously moving past it as it's not relevant to your topic. This addresses the Participants who saw the slide and desperately need to know what it was and why you moved past it. Acknowledge, then continue. Crisis averted.

In Summary:

PPTs are fantastic, but they're not what's critical for success. They're there for you as a resource, as a compliment to the data, and to ensure you're on track. They reinforce messages and create a safe environment. The PPT adds value to the learning, but should not BE the learning.

FACILITATION MYTH #5:
A SLIDE DECK MUST CONTAIN ALL THE DATA.

CHAPTER FIVE
Technology: Yes?

I fear the day that technology will surpass our human interaction. The world will have a generation of idiots.
ALBERT EINSTEIN

Technology can be a definite value-add when Facilitating. When it works, that is.

Technology can be used in pre-work, during the class and for follow-up activities. NOTE: I'm not discussing web-based, virtual training, etc. here. This book is dedicated to instructor-led Facilitation and, in this case, the use of technology supporting a live course.

Before saying another word, a key piece for the successful use of any technology is testing. TEST YOUR EQUIPMENT BEFORE YOU USE IT.

I went to an all-hands-on security meeting where a VP who was to facilitate the critical information entered a room as Participants were sitting down. It was at that moment, he decided to check to see if the video he was to play would work. Spoiler alert – it did not. The entire meeting and about 160 people needed to "come back later." He was embarrassed, everyone's time was wasted. This could have been avoided with some simple pre-work.

Let's start with pre-work. As far as pre-work goes, using technology to communicate in a timely and consistent fashion is a dream. Here, you can use and manage your survey data, update on any course changes, etc. There's no excuse for you to not know everything you need to about a student prior to a class – and, also, the student should have no reason to not know everything to be fully prepared to be on time, know the course goals, and any / all logistic details.

During the course, technology is a great way to elevate training. Some examples include:

- Videos
- Survey tech like MentiMeter, etc.
- Tablets, iPads, iPhones, etc.
- Augmented Reality (AR)
- Virtual Reality (VR)

You do NOT need to be a tech wizard to apply some of these devices. Believe me. Anyone reading this who knows me even a little has seen a copier break down at the mere whiff of my existence. I'm not great at tech, but there are some very simple solutions out there.

> Test, test, test your technology; and still always have a back-up plan for when it doesn't cooperate.

But, you DO need to have a backup for any technology you prepare to use. As sure as you're reading this, a piece of tech support will implode at some point in your communication career.

Having a backup to your technology plan is a game changer, simple to execute, and can save you from a pending disaster.

For example, if your technology fails you, here are some backup plans:

- For in-class online surveys (like MentiMeter), have your audience close their eyes and raise their hands as an answer to your questions. Then, have them open their eyes and look around the room. Flipchart the responses for added retention.

- For video, know the key pieces that need to be pulled and teach them on a flip chart with humor and animation.

- For AR or VR, this may be a really big challenge as the driving force of these mediums is to provide an "as close to reality" experience as possible. You'll need to be uber-prepared in case of a breakdown here. For example, if you're teaching about how to facilitate a surgical procedure and the plan was to use VR to walk Participants through the process and the tech breaks, you're in a pickle. With no other devices, you'll have to rely on the room – other Participants who know facets of the learnings – and use visuals as best as possible. It can be done; it's not ideal, but it can be done. The best solution here is script the AR or VR as a secondary learning piece; so if the technology doesn't work, it was never at the core of your learning material anyway.

> SEE APPENDIX (p. 170) for technology success tips.

In Summary:

Tech is great and there's no question it can add value. Practice 100 times before you use it, test the equipment, if possible have an A/V expert on hand, and always be prepared for it to just not work.

FACILITATION MYTH #6:
TECHNOLOGY ALWAYS ADDS VALUE.

STEP TWO

The ART of the Action

YOU MADE IT. You're in front of your audience. Ready. Prepared. Let's do this.

You start to feel the presence of your heart. "Can they see my chest pumping through my polo?," you ask yourself quietly. You know the material. You know your audience.

So why are my hands sweating?

Answer: Because you're human and you care.

The **ART of the Action** is where the rubber meets the road. All of your prep work helped you to successfully get to the moment where you can effectively share your materials and then allow the Learner to learn. But yet here you are, looking for a change of clothes and the exit. This feeling of wanting to flee is totally normal and natural.

At this point, the only thing that will get in the way of your success is you. Your presence, your nerves, handling hecklers, all will be tested here. Yes, it's natural to get in your own way; however, once you lean into the techniques to help guide your **ARTful** actions and keep practicing it, the unnatural will become second nature.

This section speaks to all of the tools you'll need to hone the **ART of the Action**. These tools are more than just words to say, they're also the tools to help you through the block when the words won't come or when the unexpected happens.

So, lean in, dear Reader ... here we go.

CHAPTER SIX
Where Do I Put My Hands?

The most important thing in communication is hearing what isn't said.

PETER F. DRUCKER

Have you ever seen the clip from the *Talladega Nights: The Ballad of Ricky Bobby* movie? In it, the new, successful, pro-car driver Ricky Bobby is on camera being interviewed for the first time. His voice shakes and his hands float up around his face as he states, "I'm not sure what to do with my hands." I laugh out loud every time I watch this scene because I can relate and his feelings are REAL.

Obsessing about or just being too conscious of your body can be a massive distraction for some people while speaking publicly. Nervousness can result in uncomfortable body posturing, odd tones of voice, or even a frozen stance.

This chapter isn't just literally about "where do I put my hands" while speaking. We'll focus on the importance of spatial awareness, how to use your body, how to physically communicate your message, and well, yes, to answer the question, where do I put my hands?

When we communicate a message, we do so via our *actual words*, the *tone and intonation* of our words, and *through our bodies*. If you had to guess, what percentage of communication – as in the message received by the person to whom you're talking – is made up by your words versus your body language versus your voice and tone?

The answer to this question, according to a study conducted by Albert Mehrabian and Susan R. Ferris in 1967 called *Inference of attitudes to nonverbal communication in two channels* (known as the The Mehrabian Study), the person receiving a communication trusts the element which most accurately reflects the communicator's true feelings towards them. From the studies, it appears that more is conveyed by the nonverbal clues than by the spoken word. Most psychologists agree that the majority of the messages we "hear" are received non-verbally; i.e. body language and tone of voice.

> Trust in messages comes through these channels:
> - 7% words
> - 55% body language
> - 38% tone and information

While there is some criticism to the exactness behind the study, the interpretation that I trust and the specific answer to the aforementioned question is as follows: **7% of trust in messages comes through words, 55% through body language, and 38% through tone and intonation.**

As a Facilitator, we need to understand this theory to ensure we're communicating with our entire selves, not just the words from our mouths. What this research addresses is when the nonverbal and verbal messages were perceived to be incongruent, your audience loses trust. You've lost your credibility and it no longer matters how valid your message is because your audience doesn't believe in you.

We're not going to spend any time on words here – when you know your material, the words will come. The critical focus for this chapter is on your body and intonation/tone.

Let's start with body language. By now, you've probably learned about body language on some level. And I'm sure you've experienced the interpretation of a message by merely people-watching at some point in your life.

Think about a time when you were out to dinner and, out of your periphery, you saw the couple a few tables away. You couldn't hear what they were saying, but it was clear they were not getting along and having a poor time together. Or, think about the last time you were at the airport and you watched a happy family getting ready to board a plane. Again, you couldn't hear their words, but you knew from their posturing and smiles and eye contact that they were excited and ready to go.

Body language can be conveyed and can help to maintain consistency of your messaging through some of the following examples:

- Eye contact
- Finger pointing versus an open palm
- Moving throughout your space
- Removal of "nervous tics"
- Standing versus sitting
- Using or not using a podium
- Your posture and stance
- Facial expression
- Hips and shoulders (facing toward or at an angle to the person to whom you are speaking)

It's clear that body language is critical when you're Facilitating a conversation to show that you're engaged with the group and interested in their responses.

Did you know, you can also use your body to illustrate a message or to make a specific point?

For example, when I transition from one topic to another while communicating, I oftentimes exaggerate my body and move it from one side of the room or the stage to the other. This physically demonstrates the act of separating topics. Another example is how a Facilitator can gesture with an open palm to the ceiling, asking the room to look up at the invisible "thing" to which he or she is teaching. The point is, your body is not this lifeless boring obstacle standing in the way of your communicating – you are physically a part of the message so use this incredible prop to your advantage and use it however and whenever you can.

Body posturing that is not okay:

- Standing with arms crossed translates that you're closed off.

- Standing with arms crossed behind your back also closes you off.

- Hands in your pockets. You can, however, put your hand in a pocket after you earn some trust. Then, later, putting one hand in a pocket shows comfort and casualness. Be careful to not do it for exaggerated periods of time or to make it a habit. If you have change or keys in your pocket, then absolutely never put your hands in your pocket. (But really, don't carry change or keys in your pockets when Facilitating anyway!)

> When your nonverbal and verbal messages are incongruent, your audience loses trust. Be comfortable, be authentic, be you.

- Sitting all the time. If you're Facilitating a "true" course, you're not sitting. You're up, using the room, and commanding the space. You can absolutely sit when the time is right. For example, if the class is having a deep conversation around something, you can pull up a chair to send the message you are listening and have become one of them. Then it's okay to sit. For the most part, if you're Facilitating, send the message of authority by standing.

- Only standing at the top of the room. If you're presenting to a CEO in a boardroom, most likely you must stay at the top of the conference table, unless you're 100% sure of your audience. However, if you can use your space, be sure to do so and walk the entire room. This ensures all participants are acknowledged and, because people will have to shift in their seats to see you, it promotes physical engagement to help with retention.

- Standing behind a podium. If you're Facilitating a commencement speech at your alma mater, then you may have to. However, if you have the chance to get out from behind anything including a podium, remove all barriers between you and your audience.

- Pacing. This is a common occurrence. While trying to use the "top" of the room, we walk back and forth and create a distraction for the audience. Most novices do this while pacing right in front of a screen, also creating distraction. It's better to stay in one place for a significant amount of time than to pace.

- Having loose or distracting clothing, jewelry, or even hair. No need to add any more distractions – put your hair up and away, lose the scarves, and remove anything that can hang or make noise (like keys in your pocket).

Body posturing that is okay:

- Using the room and walking the space.
- Smiling. Often and always!

- Using your arms and hands to gesture. Yes. Whatever is comfortable and natural to you.

- Leaning back on a wall or on a table. After you've set the tone of the experience and if you're debriefing a module or an exercise, leaning is okay. Just be conscious and don't stay that way throughout the entire experience.

- Kneeling down at a table during a team exercise. This posture is a great way to humble yourself to your audience and get to their level to lend support through the learning process.

It's also important to know that different cultures and different countries can interpret body language differently. For example, pointing, which in most places in the US would be acceptable would absolutely NOT be perceived well in China, amongst other countries. The key to presenting with impact is understanding the nuances of your audience and cultural expectations, and being respectful of that.

Some interpretations of gestures from around the world are as follows:

GESTURE	MEANING
Thumbs up	Sit on it. Australia, Greece, Middle East
Peace sign (palm facing in)	Up yours. We're excellent at archery. Australia, United Kingtom, South Africa
Talk to the hand	I've had enough. Greece, Mexico, Africa, Middle East
A-OK	A-hole. Greece, Spain, Brazil

GESTURE		MEANING
🤘	Rock on!	Your wife is sleeping with someone else. Spain, Italy, Greece
👈	Come hither	You are a dog (and come here). Philippines, Slovakia, East Asia, Singapore
🤞	Good luck!	Lady parts. Vietnam
👉	Pointing	Used to indicate an inanimate object. China, Japan, Indonesia, Latin America

To directly answer the question, where do I put my hands, the answer is: wherever you would normally put them. The point is, be you, be comfortable, and get out of your head about it. If you're not normally demonstrative and moving about, that's okay. Just be you up there.

Now let's focus on your voice – the tone and intonation in which you speak. To make this point, read the following sentences out loud and put verbal focus on the highlighted/capitalized word:

- I **NEVER** said I'd meet you at the restaurant.
- I never **SAID** I'd meet you at the restaurant.
- I never said I'd **MEET** you at the restaurant.
- I never said I'd meet **YOU** at the restaurant.
- I never said I'd meet you at the **RESTAURANT**.

Overall, your Participants can sense insincerity when tone is incongruent with words. My mother used to say to me all the time growing up, "it's not what you're saying, it's how you're saying it." (Ironically, her tone was quite clear when she would say that.) I never really understood the importance of her message until I was older and heard my first incongruent "I love you." Ouch. You know it when you hear a tone that doesn't align with your words and the audience to whom you're delivering will certainly hear it too.

What happens when you're on the phone and trying to communicate your message?

Most of the communication is voice and tone. Body language is still important, however. For example, most people can tell over the phone if you're smiling. Years ago, I trained inside sales teams on selling cable boxes and programs via telemarketing. The first thing I did was to give all the employees mirrors for their desks with the words "smile" imprinted on them. Yes, some of them used the mirrors to check their makeup, but for most, seeing themselves was a subtle reminder to smile. The point is you can hear a smile even over the phone.

> SEE APPENDIX (p. 163) for a Body Language checklist and (p. 164) for a Gestures checklist matching game.

Control what you can control and do everything you can to project your message with authenticity and positivity.

What about emails?

We discussed sending emails to communicate via prework and to set expectations to reduce the tension of our Participants. Knowing that you can't control the filter in which your Participant is reading your words is very, very important. Email communication only uses words, which can easily lead to confusion.

Sarcasm often doesn't translate over email.

An email is not the time to try and be funny and cutesy; it just won't translate. Yes, if you are sure of your recipient and can add a smiley face with words like "just kidding," then it could be okay. But, why even take the chance. Keep emails short, concise, and straightforward. If you're sending information regarding one of your experiences, why clutter the message with any potential miscommunication.

In Summary:

Where do I put my hands? The answer is, do what comes natural. Being natural will come from being confident in what you're communicating and allowing yourself to be AUTHENTIC in your tone, body, and words. If you're confident, your hands will take care of themselves. Holding something can help if you use it to gesture and point; however if you're nervous and your hands shake, my recommendation is to not hold anything that can rattle or make noise (like a piece of paper). It will add to your concern about where to put your hands and not aid you at all.

Regardless of where you put your body, know that you do a lot of communicating with body language and tone and your Participants will look for congruency across all three components: the words you say, your tone, and your body language.

Be aware, use your space and be you.

FACILITATION MYTH #7:
SUCCESSFUL COMMUNICATION IS ALL ABOUT WHAT YOU SAY.

CHAPTER SEVEN
I'm Freaking Out! Why Am I So Nervous?

There are two types of speakers: those who get nervous and those who are liars.

MARK TWAIN

This is normal.

It's normal to feel nervous or scared before you present. If you didn't, I would think there's something wrong with you. Or, that you're an android.

To move forward, you have to accept you'll probably always be nervous before you launch a course, or make a speech, or present an idea. I still get nerves and I have been speaking publicly for my entire adult life. To this day when I start speaking to an audience my hands shake and I can't hold anything until I settle. But the good news is, you can conquer nerves; you can do it with actions and, more importantly, you can do it with conscious thought.

You see, what you are feeling as you step out on that stage, is anxiety. Our definition of anxiety is, "experiencing failure before it happens." Let that sink in. All of the shaking, the negative thought, the hyperventilating, and the sweating is coming

> Anxiety, as discussed here, is defined as "experiencing failure before it happens." While we address nervousness as a normal part of public speaking, any concerns related with anxiety disorders should be discussed and treated with a medical professional.

from your mind experiencing what probably won't even happen. You've concocted a story around a worst-case scenario.

Occasional anxiety is an expected part of life. This book, however, does not address concerns related with anxiety disorders. Those should be discussed and treated with a medical professional.

It's normal and natural and we all do it. But, now you know what's happening and you can adjust. Break the cycle and brush away the anxiety to the point that gets you to that stage.

To prove that anxiety is experienced by all mortals, let's learn from Will Smith, the entertainer. As the story goes, Will decided to jump out of an airplane (on purpose) with some friends and family. He did so during an evening party where emotions and adrenaline were running rampant.

> SEE APPENDIX (p. 166–167) for tips on handling nerves.

Later that evening, after commitments were made, while alone in his bed, he started to experience his fear. His fear of the jump, the fall, impending death, etc. He couldn't sleep and he couldn't stop experiencing his worst-case scenario.

Fast forward to the day of his jump where his experience was ultimately positive and as a result, he had an epiphany around his anxiety and fear. He realized that he wasted energy and time over consciously thinking about what could happen. He said, "The point of maximum danger, is the point of minimum fear. In that moment ... when you should be the most terrified, it's the most blissful experience of your life. God placed the best things in life on the other side of fear."
(youtube.com/watch?v+gG-F_rRVdLc).

He experienced anxiety, just like the rest of us. All of the anxiety and negative thinking about what could happen the weeks and days before an event is a waste – what good does that bring you? We can actually replace the negative thoughts with those of excitement for the success we're about to experience. This can be learned to the point where we train ourselves to adjust; to brush away the anxiety and replace it with something else.

To do this, there are tactics we can deploy before a speaking event, just before an event, and during an event.

BEFORE THE EVENT

ONE: *Visualize*

Yes, you've heard this before. Did you know that almost every successful athlete engages in the **ART** of visualization; not just minutes before an event, but for months and months prior?

It's real and it works.

Visualizing is not just used in sports psychology, but this is where it gets the most and the best press. Athletes and their coaches believe, "What happens out there is a result of what happens in here." In simple terms, this means outward performance is often the result of what's happening inside your head.

The brain doesn't differentiate between a real memory and an imagined (or visualized) one. When you imagine vividly and with energy, you actually change the chemistry in your brain as though the experience was real. Because of this characteristic of the mind, we can use visualization to overcome fear and build self-confidence by making the unknown known.

This was discovered by physiologist Edmund Jacobson when he had subjects visualize certain athletic activities.

Through the use of sensitive detection instruments, he discovered subtle but very real movements in the muscles that corresponded to the movement the muscles would make if they were really performing the imagined activity.

Further research revealed that a person who consistently visualizes a certain physical skill develops "muscle memory," which helps him when he physically engages in the activity. A related study by Australian psychologist Alan Richardson confirmed the reality of this phenomenon.

In his study, Richardson chose to focus on the sport of basketball and the specific activity of making free throws. He chose three groups of students at random, none of whom had ever practiced visualization. The first group practiced free throws every day for twenty days. The second made free throws only on the first day and the twentieth day, as did the third group. But, members of the third group spent 20 minutes every day visualizing free throws. While visualizing, if they "missed," they "practiced" getting the next shot right.

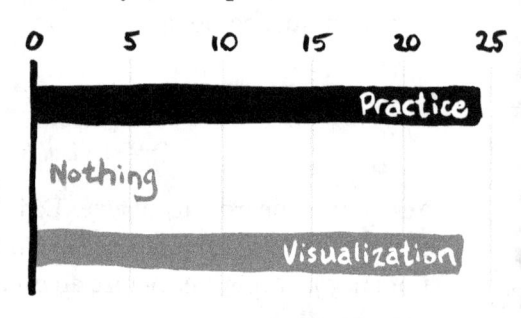

On the twentieth day, Richardson measured the percentage of improvement in each group. The group that practiced daily improved 24 percent. The second group, unsurprisingly, improved not at all. The third group, which had physically practiced no more than the second, did 23 percent better – almost as well as the first group.

In his paper on the experiment, published in Research Quarterly, Richardson wrote that the most effective visualization occurs when the visualizer feels and sees what he is doing. In other words, the visualizers in the basketball experiment "felt" the ball in their hands and "heard" it bounce, in addition to "seeing" it go through the hoop.

When we visualize an action, the same regions of the brain are stimulated as when we perform it and the same neural networks are created. This explains why visualization is part of most world-class athletes' training: because it works.

TWO: *Practice*

The most amazing Facilitators you've experienced have honed their crafts. Like athletes, they practice, practice and practice. They continue to try new skills even when they know they're already confident in their **ARTful** delivery.

However, don't over practice. Have you ever seen a rehearsed comic? One who tells the joke – and it's a funny joke – but, the delivery is so rote that it's actually no longer funny. Over rehearsing can lead to mediocrity and can also lead to banality. There's so much that comes from being in the moment and seeing where the audience and the course materials take you.

When I worked for Volkswagen in the late 90s, I was teaching the same three courses literally every week for months. I had to work very hard to keep the material fresh – not just for the audience, but for me. There were times, however, I found myself in such a pattern and routine that I was able to be talking and setting up an activity while at the same time thinking, "did I lock my front door today?" I'm sure the audience that day did not get the best Tina they could as my mind was elsewhere as I was not doing my best to stretch, grow and challenge myself to try new techniques.

Practice until you feel you are confident with the material, but not to the point where you know every single word you'll say during a six-hour experience. Keep it fresh, keep it flowing, keep it authentic.

THREE: *Know Your Audience*

Learn as much as you can about the people with whom you'll be leading; really consider the reality of people's lives and acknowledge it early on or all of your efforts could be moot.

Questions to know about your audience:

- Does your audience want to be there or are they "prisoners," forced to be there by their boss or management?

- What is going on for them in the real world that may come up in the class?

- What realities need to be acknowledged before we start? i.e. perhaps the company to whom you're teaching is going through a merger, but the class topic is about internal processes. The reality of the organizational situation should be acknowledged up front.

- Do you have different levels of seniority in a group? Different teams?

- What's the relationship/dynamic, etc.?

The more you know about your Participants, the better you can prepare. Remember, control what you can control. This is an element most other Facilitators don't explore and can find themselves caught off guard. When preparing, always do your research prior and plan accordingly. As a result, you may need to start your experience acknowledging the elephant in the room; and then you'll have an audience who is willing to listen and participate.

FOUR: *Prepare YOU*

We spoke at length regarding what you can do to ensure your Participants have an ideal experience – through preparation, communication, setup, etc. But, what about you?

In the days and nights prior to your experience, be sure you've taken care of your personal self. Ensure you don't have anything else to worry about and can focus your attention on the matter at hand, your course, your delivery, and your people.

Start by confirming your personal logistics are handled:

- Confirm all the logistics for your Participants are handled and communicated.
- Pack your bag early.
- Know where you're going. Hotel, flights, foods, etc.
- Know how are you getting to and from.
- Who are your Participants? What is their contact info in case you need to communicate with them?
- If something goes wrong, who do you contact and what's the process?
- Does all of your technology work and do you have backup if it goes south during the gig?

If you've taken care of your personal business prior to starting your event, you'll be that much more focused and able to put your attention on your business at hand.

MINUTES AND HOURS BEFORE THE EVENT

ONE: *Walk the Room*

Literally be in the space where you will facilitate as soon as you can and as often as you can. The more you "live" in the space, the more your body will adjust, and your confidence level will raise.

As your Participants enter your room and as they gather, continue to stand and be in your Facilitation space; as if the Participants are just becoming an extension of your own comfort zone.

The more you are literally in the space where you'll facilitate, the more "at home" you'll become, and the more relaxed you'll be.

TWO: *Breathe*

I know you know to breathe. However, when we panic, we naturally hold our breath, yet are unaware. Have you ever been in a tight situation and all of a sudden realized your body had no oxygen; and then you took a huge breath to fill your lungs? This sounds a tad obvious but, your brain needs oxygen to work. When we hold our breath, we don't think straight and, as a result, we are unable to skillfully brush the fear away. Breathe. Remember to breathe.

You need to breathe and breathe consciously to help ensure your nerves don't get the best of you.

When breathing consciously to relax, a tactic I use that works is called "straw breathing." Pretend you have a straw (not a plastic one, a biodegradable one – even though it's invisible, it doesn't mean we can't be responsible) tucked under your top lip so it hangs down in front of your mouth like a long walrus tooth. By doing this, your top lip will extend just a bit over your bottom lip providing a small space to expel air.

Take a deep breath in through your nose, hold it for a moment, and then blow it out through the "straw" slowly and consciously. This act will reduce your heart rate, provide oxygen, and calm your body. As you're doing this, use your visualization techniques to mentally paint the picture of what you're about to say and the smiles on the audience's faces. Feel your smile and how your body reacts to the smile. Do this all while breathing – which only needs to take a minute or two. The more you do it, the more quickly you'll relax.

Just breathe.

THREE: *Smile*

Ready for this – the mere act of smiling tricks the body into becoming happy. The trigger of a smile activates neural messaging and releases boosting neuropeptides that work towards fighting off stress.

Neuropeptides are tiny molecules that allow neurons to communicate – regardless of the message: happy, sad, angry, depressed, etc. However, the "feel good" neurotransmitters – dopamine, endorphins, and serotonin – are all released when a smile flashes across your face. This not only relaxes your body, but it can also lower your heart rate and blood pressure.

Don't tell the pharmaceutical industry, but by smiling, the release of serotine alone serves as an anti-depressant or mood lifter. Many of the prescribed pharma antidepressants influence this same chemical release.

On top of how your brain reacts to a smile, a 2011 finding by researchers at the Face Research Laboratory at the University of Aberdeen, Scotland, found a direct correlation between smiling and attractiveness. Subjects found that both men and women were more attracted to images of people who made eye contact and smiled than those who did not. According to a study published in the journal *Neuropsychologia*, when you see an attractive, smiling person, this activates the region in your brain that processes sensory rewards. When you see a person smiling, you actually feel rewarded.

Give us a smile. You'll be happy and they'll feel rewarded. It's a win/win!

FOUR: Talk with Participants

A Facilitator will often ignore their guests, regardless of the setting, in order to focus on what they're about to say or do. While you might feel compelled to continue to prepare up until minutes before you begin your event, there comes a point when the focus needs to shift to the Participants in the room.

The more you bond and interact with your guests, the more of a tension reduction you'll provide them. In turn, their relaxed energy will affect you positively. When it's time for you to start talking, you'll have an immediate connection with almost everyone allowing you to approach them as friends and not strangers.

FIVE: Know and Remind Yourself – They Have No Clue What I'm About to Say/Do

Literally. They don't have a clue. You could start to talk about zebras in a class entitled *How to Tie a Slip Knot* and the participants wouldn't know you just flubbed.

There's so much power in this fact. Just before you start any speech, keynote, class, or presentation, remember that the audience has no clue what your plan is. Therefore, if you mess up, only YOU know. Remind yourself of this little gem as you're saying good morning; you'll be surprised as how empowered you'll feel and how the nerves will slip away.

DURING THE EVENT

ONE: Make Them Laugh

Personally, I use laughter immediately and often. It's proven that the result of laughter is an immediate release, a tension reduction in the body, which replaces nerves. I swear, as soon as I get the first laugh, I feel my body's tension melt away.

Laughter triggers the brain to deliver a bucket of dopamine (the feel-good hormone) and serotonin, which lifts your mood. Laughter can even increase the release of endorphins, the pain-relieving chemical normally associated with exercise, food, and sex.

Worried about being funny? Don't be – everyone can be funny, even if it's scripted or rehearsed (not too much) just to get you started. Self-deprecation (when not overused) is an ideal and easy way to get a little empathy, a laugh, and is also a tension reduction. Once, I actually created a presentation with a spelling error just so I could stop and say, "Does that say Ledership instead of Leadership? Good thing this isn't a spelling class." Okay, it's not hysterical, but it humanized me to the Participants and created enough dopamine release to relax everyone in the room. You can do this.

TWO: *Hydrate*

There are studies that show being dehydrated can increase cortisol levels, which are your stress hormones. Drinking water – not coffee, or soda, or energy drinks – will keep your stress levels down. Don't get me wrong, I adore espresso, but on days I facilitate, I keep the caffeine intake low knowing my adrenalin will be the elixir of the day to get me through.

If the body is not properly hydrated, it will mimic real anxiety issues and could cause dizziness, muscle fatigue, headache, feeling faint, increased heart rate or nausea. These feelings could trick your mind and possibly trigger a panic attack.

Conversely, drinking water can be soothing and often your body will benefit from the added hydration during times of intense stress like standing up in front of 30 people. In a 2009 study, Tufts University found a clear link between hydration and mood. Scientists found that student athletes who were just mildly dehydrated reported feeling angry, confused, tense, and fatigued.

These days, I have taken to carrying around a reusable water bottle with a metal straw attached to it, even when not facilitating. For some reason, I drink more water as a result and consider my bottle an everyday accessory. Control what you can control and if simply drinking water will help increase your game, why not do it?

THREE: *Slow Down Your Speech*

Anyone reading this who knows me personally, is laughing hysterically right now. I don't do slow, especially when I'm talking. I taught a class in Atlanta in 1999 to 30 automotive sales people and after five minutes of talking, a man leaned out from his seat. With a kind face and the sweetest southern accent he said, "Tina Darling – we haven't understood a word you said for the past five minutes, can you start over?"

Yes. That happened.

When we get nervous, we speak even more rapidly perpetuating a vicious cycle. The mere act of consciously slowing down your output, will slow you, and ultimately relax you while you're facilitating.

It might not be easy, but with a conscious effort, it can be done and the end-results will be well worth it.

FOUR: *Be Aware; the Reaction to the Nerves*

Remember, it's about your Participants experience and not about you. Your audience has no clue what is "supposed" to happen. If you make a mistake, it's best to just go with it.

However sometimes, when we allow our nerves to get the best of us, our automatic response is to compensate, and the result is not always positive. Filler Funnies and Whisker Words are natural compensation techniques that Facilitators should try to avoid.

1. Filler Funnies: These are those bad jokes or statements we make when we flub, forget, or fall. Don't get me wrong, being funny is an amazing tool during Facilitation. I've leaned on this tool often and frequently. However, if you are humiliated, embarrassed, or just feel lost and you try to make a joke and try too hard, this results in a Filler Funny: a joke that falls flat.

> SEE APPENDIX (p. 165) for a worksheet on Filler Funnies, Whisker Words, and Silence.

For example, I was facilitating to a group of technicians and I said "...and if you **do do** that ..." I was nervous and my immediate Filler Funny was, "... did you hear that, I just said do-do." Yes, I said "do-do" to a room full of adults because my nerves got to me. Luckily I was forgiven quickly, but I'll never forget how I compromised the integrity of the class and my own credibility by leaning into my nerves.

You're going to make mistakes. How you respond, instead of react, is part of the **ART** of what you're learning here. Instead of immediately trying to "fix" or "cover" for your mistake, replace the Filler Funny with a breath or an extended pause. Most of the time, your Filler Funny will fall flat anyway and it's better to have let your Participants think you're nervous, then to try and fix it with a Filler Funny. My Grandfather always said, "even a fish wouldn't get caught if he kept his mouth shut." Take a pause, self correct and move on.

2. **Whisker Words:** Imagine asking a thoughtful question to a man with a beard. As he begins to create his answer, he lifts his head to the sky, takes a deep breath, starts to thoughtfully stroke his beard, and lets out a long sigh followed by an extended "hmmmmm." That "hmmmm" is his Whisker Word, and the visual of the man stroking his whiskers is where the term got its name. A Whisker Word is a word, statement, or sound that the Facilitator leans on when thinking of what to say next.

   "Um" is by far the strongest and most widely used Whisker Word. We humans are not fans of silence; we don't like dead air. Therefore, as we think or react with nervousness, we insert an UMMMM instead of just leaving the space alone. It's natural, normal and, everyone does it.

   The word "like" is quickly catching up to the word "um." The use of the word "like" is a big pet peeve of mine. Perhaps it's because I grew up in the 80's when the word "like" was part of the popular slang of the day. I'm hoping we can all agree to leave "like" back in the 80's where it belongs.

   Phrases can be Whisker Words as well. During a large product launch for BMW in 2005 I was the Lead Facilitator and I was tasked with ensuring the audience was excited and enthusiastic. My Whisker Word phrase became, "Now that's what I'm talking about!" I had no idea I was even saying it but apparently I said it many, many times. At the end of the morning, a friend and fellow Facilitator approached me with a hand written sheet noting all the times I had said the phrase; and he was laughing uncontrollably. Whisker Words are normal and the game changer is knowing yours and wiping them out.

   How to wipe them out? A good technique to help Facilitators curb the habit of using Whisker Words is to create a grounding reminder. Choose a piece of jewelry that you always wear – a watch, a ring, whatever – and put it on another part of yourself. For example, wear your watch on the opposite wrist or place your ring on a different finger. By doing this, you are creating a physical reminder of something and you'll be continuously aware.

> Create a grounding technique to wipe out the habit of using Whisker Words.

Your conscious mind will attach the new physical feeling to your Whisker Word and will remind you not to use it. It will get to the point where you'll forget about the watch on the "wrong" wrist, your subconscious mind will take over, and you'll begin to not use your word. This technique is effective and it's worked for many people. Try it as it'll work for you too.

In Summary:

You are going to have strong emotions when it comes to facilitating your message. Know that everyone around you is in the same boat. You may not have time for the nerves, but they'll come. And now you know how to work with them.

The more you practice the **ART of Facilitation**, while the nerves will always be there when you start, you'll be amazed at how quickly you use them, move through them, and ultimately lose them as you continue through your experience.

The Greeks had a word for this – called *apatheia:* the "freedom or release from emotion or excitement." It's a state of mind and a skill set that takes practice and repetition. Continue to replace the nervous thought with another and move on – you'll get there.

FACILITATION MYTH #8:
PROS DON'T GET NERVOUS.

CHAPTER EIGHT
Actually Doing It

*Tell me and I forget. Show me and I remember.
Involve me and I understand.*

CHINESE PROVERB

The **ART of Facilitation** is not about telling, it's about involving and asking.

There are a few techniques I'm going to share, but if you take nothing else from this chapter, take this critical point: being able to ask open-ended, thought provoking questions may be the #1 game changing characteristic for an **ARTful Facilitator**.

We will get to the **ART** of asking questions soon. Before we get there, we must address what leads up to the question – and this is the **ART** of the design and flow of your content.

The flow of any **ARTful** communication usually follows the pattern of: tell the audience what you're going to tell them, tell them the material, and tell them what you told them. (The how of the "telling them" we will get to, but this is your basic flow when facilitating.)

The design of the class is paramount and once you know that you've designed the right flow by ensuring you're teaching to all learning types, you're ready to go. While this book is about Facilitating **ARTfully**, not designing **ARTfully**, it's still important to know the core principles of content development to maintain a good balance and a high level of participation.

Let's have a quick chat about some content design principles here as you may be creating the content you're facilitating and not just facilitating someone else's material.

That said, the template here follows the ultimate content development process of:

- Preparation
- Presentation
- Practice
- Performance

Preparation	Presentation
Practice	Performance

Preparation: It's critical to ensure you've sowed your seeds to create an environment of controlling stress reduction and preparing the Learner to learn. **We've discussed preparing for your event at length in earlier chapters.**

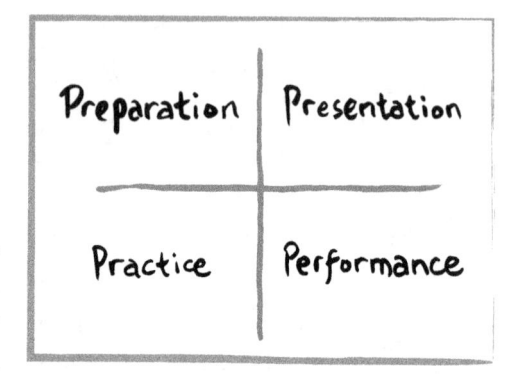

Presentation and Practice: These middle components are the key to the **ART of Facilitation** as demonstrated in this book. A Facilitator's goal is to reach 20% of their time presenting materials, and 80% of their time ensuring Participants practice the materials presented.

Put simply, presenting is talking about a topic at hand, setting up an activity by giving directions or debriefing an activity that has just occurred.

Practice includes actions performed by the student to create their own data. This is where the magic happens and we want to spend as much time while Facilitating to get our Participants to do the work for themselves.

Honestly, reaching 80% Practice and 20% Presentation is challenging. I find myself at 35%/65% (Presentation/Practice) on a good day; and that's just fine. If you're ensuring the student creates his/her own data for the most part, then you're on the right track and your experience will most likely be stellar.

Performance: After the event, the performance piece is all about the follow-up and assurance that your materials "stuck." This piece occurs after you've done your job, after the experience is over, and where you're looking to ensure an ROI (return on investment). We won't focus on the activities to ensure "stickablity" of materials post class as, again, our focus is purely on live Facilitation. But, know that the performance piece is a critical piece of the overall training picture if you're in the business of developing training.

FOCUS ON THE FLOW

In order to shoot for an 80%/20% or 70%/30% balance, here is an actual flow for a solid day of Facilitation that can be your "talking-template" for success:

- Introduction of the course and you.
- Communicate the logistic details. Give them that tension reduction and be sure they know food will come, where the bathrooms are, etc. Set expectations and let them know they're safe – this is critical.
- Share the class objectives. No more than three.
- Intro and facilitate the opening activity; build group relationships, set the stage.
- Debrief
- Setup/facilitate the next point
- Activity
- Debrief
- Setup/facilitate the next point. Ensure linearity to previous data points.
- Activity

- Debrief
- Setup/facilitate the next point. Continue to be linear in thought.
- Activity
- Debrief
- Final activity putting a bow on the day
- "Stick-ability" activity. Give them a call to action; something that allows them to have a personal take-away. This is critical to show the purpose for their engagement in your experience.

This "talking-template" is just that, a generic template. It's an ideal communication flow to showcase the cadence of how a Facilitated message can be received successfully. Now that you have this high level overview, we can dive into how you will **ARTfully** navigate the actual Facilitation of this flow.

DOING IT

ONE: *Asking Questions*

Using questions is a game changer to elevating your Facilitation skills. Questions can be used even during the presentation phase of your flow to continue to support the 80%/20% rule and encourage participation, even when you're doing the sharing.

So, why don't we use this skill more? Why do we as humans just not use questioning techniques in general; especially in a learning environment when a Student asks US a question? The answer: as you learned in the introduction, humans want to naturally FIX. And, somewhere along the way we decided that if we've been asked to professionally Facilitate, we must have all the answers, must answer all the questions, and can fix any situation. We have been taught that we will be judged, looked down upon, and seen as having no value if we don't answer the question at hand. This simply is not the truth.

After all your years of answering questions and giving answers, breaking your habit won't be easy. It will take a lot of conscious practice and effort. To prove it, let's try a little experiment.

Right now, please stand up and cross your arms in front of your chest. Next, take the arm on the bottom and reverse the fold and put the bottom arm on the top.

How does that feel? How challenging was it to reverse your arms per my instruction? How comfortable are you in this moment?

It probably feels weird. It was a challenge to reverse your arms and you had to take conscious thought to make it happen. You actually had to THINK about folding your arms, and now you're not comfortable – you're actually UNcomfortable.

> Asking questions is the #1 component that differentiates presenters from Facilitators – from "that was ok" to "that was an amazing experience."

This is exactly how it will feel to consciously change your approach and use questioning as a daily technique. I say daily as I would challenge you to use questioning in your every day life, not just when you're communicating your message as a Facilitator. It took me years to be able to master the ability to NOT answer a question when asked. Again, humans are programmed to fix; they want to help and give and heal others. We want to be validated and feel good about ourselves. By providing answers, we check all of these internal/intrinsic needs that again, have been programmed within.

There's some other motivators for just answering a Participant's question. Like, "I too want to be the smart guy."

"I want to get to the answer and just move on." "I want to get credit for fixing you!"

I have learned that all of our motivators to give the answer are real and valid, but when you lean into the desire to just "tell," you lose it all – your value, credibility, and the Participant's engagement and absorption of information.

There are two ways to use questions to get your message across:

- The Question-Back
- The Conscious Participation-Question

The Question Back

The **ART** of the "question back" is a learned skill. Once mastered, it's literally a game-changer. When I mastered it, I went from being completely depleted at the end of a day to feeling rejuvenated, because I was Facilitating smart, not hard.

Your Audience WANTS to be heard. Let them do the work, feel great about themselves and get *you* out of the way of *their* learning.

The question back is simple: when you're asked a question, turn that question over to the room. Simply pause and say …

"That's a great question. Does *anyone* know the answer to the question?"

Boom. Mic drop.

I am saying that when asked a question, you as the Facilitator DON'T answer. Allowing your audience to participate in this way is a huge gift for them AND you.

What value does this bring?

Number one – it ensures you won't have laryngitis at the end of a day. I'm serious. Again, why are you working so hard? Why is it in our DNA to feel the need to have all the answers? When you turn the floor over to others, you allow yourself to have an incredible break and lessen the strain on your body and mind.

Number two – wow, will your audience feel great. In the chapter to come about Hecklers, we talk about folks who are desperate to show how smart they are. This doesn't only hold true to Hecklers; everyone wants to be acknowledged and validated. By flipping a question back to your audience, it allows them to get a chance to be valued and complimented for their participation.

Number three – it can spark amazing conversation and open up your experience to become even more valuable. Yes, your job is to keep your event on track. However, if you're leading a group and an elevated conversation happens as a result of your question back and your **ARTful Facilitation**, then yippee. Be happy about the left turn – yes you have to lead it appropriately and not let it get so off topic you can't bring it back, but go for it and enjoy the ride as the learning will occur.

Some other examples of the question back are:

- "Who feels comfortable answering that?"

- "Hmm … interesting question … tell me more about that." (Not really a question *per se*, but will open up the person who is asking to talk and share more. This is a real winner. Use this with anyone at any time and it will reveal a whole host of information.)

- "Who can add to that?" (Use this when a Participant is making more of a statement than asking a question.)

Some rules for questions in general:

- **Be clear and concise.** State your question in as few words as possible.

- **One at a time – no stacking.** Stacking is asking more than question at a time. This is a bad habit and many of us have it. Watch the morning interview television shows and take notice of the interviewers. At times, even the professionals stack their questions and it drives the person who is being interviewed to only answer the last question, because that's what he/she remembers. To avoid this, ask a single question at a time, get a response, and then continue. Don't ask multiple questions at once or you'll risk confusing the audience.

- **Wait for the answer.** Not all good questions can be answered immediately. And sometimes, you just didn't ask it well. Get comfortable with a few seconds of silence after you ask a question. Avoid jumping in and clarifying or changing the question right away. Give people a chance to process.

- **Rephrase or clarify.** If you did indeed ask a question poorly, wait a beat – then state, "Okay, let me rephrase …" and ask again with clarity. Put the error on you.

These rules will help you ask great questions. But, what do you do if you ask the perfect question and get an incorrect response?

I've had student Facilitators tell me straight out, "I don't ask question because I'm afraid of getting the wrong answer."

I love getting the wrong answer. This provides such a wonderful learning ground for everyone. The key here is you HAVE to handle it immediately and with grace.

What you never, never, ever do is to say, "You're wrong." Or, "well that's just silly." Never negate the answer right off the bat even if it's categorically wrong. What will happen is your Participant will shut down and not participate for the rest of the day and, others will be terrified to take a chance at answering any future questions. As a result, you'll ruin any momentum you've built. So, turn the focus away from the group and back to you.

> Don't fear a wrong answer from a Participant. Facilitated well, it can be a great opportunity for group learning.

When a person answers you incorrectly, here's some options:

1. **Acknowledge.** You should always say "thanks" when someone gives you something. An answer to your question is a gift, even if it's wrong. Acknowledge the attempt by using phrasing like, "I see how you could approach it that way." Or even a simple, "Ok, thanks for the input." The key is to ensure the Participant leaves with a feeling that their attempt was valued regardless of the correctness.

2. **Ask the group.** Now, you need to "fix" the answer. Chances are, somebody in the group will recognize the wrong information and will be happy to jump in and help you fix it. This makes it a group project, which again focuses on others. You can simply ask, "Does anyone have anything to add?" Or even, "What do you think of John's idea?" to get the conversation moving. Always honor the source and return to the original student at the end of the conversation. Ask if he or she can see the difference.

3. **"Yes, and."** This is an improv technique used to carry a scene forward. It allows you to build on what's there and add your information. This is a simple as saying "Yes, I can see how you came to that conclusion, and to add to that, …" If we say "but" as opposed to "and" to the

Participant, anything prior to the BUT is negated and, therefore, the acknowledgment is erased. (You'll learn a tad more about this technique in the next few pages.)

Your overall goal when addressing a wrong answer is to maintain a safe learning environment for all, while ensuring the correct information is shared and learned throughout.

What happens when there's no answer? What happens when there's the dreaded silence?

Silence.

Scary.

Silence is not a bad thing. Silence is your friend. Allow it. Allow your Participants to think and contemplate and process. After you ask a question, trust your gut as to how long is too long for the silence and then interject. Perhaps a, "let me rephrase the question" is necessary. Someone will inevitable answer and if not, then you take the lead and get the class back on track. Never ruin a chance for some good silence.

The Conscious Participation Question

These are questions that you've either scripted ahead of time to encourage dialogue or questions you've created on the spot to get folks engaged.

For these questions, they should be open-ended to inspire the most dialogue. While closed-ended questions have value and have a time and place, most of the time you'll want to live in the world of open-ended questions that allow for audience engagement.

That said, right now take out a piece of paper. Write down the word DO. Now, draw a circle around it and cross a line through it. Humans have started questions with the word "do" forever. We are just **predisposed** to do this and after you start a question with DO, you almost always get a yes or no. Then, you're stuck. Try to remove this word from your questioning vocabulary and replace it with the following starter words/phrases:

- Why ...
- How ...
- Tell me about a time when ...
- Who can share their experience around ...

The open-ended question is a true gift that allows you to be in "Presentation Mode" and get your message across while still ensuring there is Participant engagement; allowing people to continue to create their own data while you're sharing yours.

When do you use a close-ended question? When you want a close-ended answer, of course. There are times when you need this. For example:

- When you are presenting but you want some quick engagement, raise your hand and ask others to raise theirs as well (engaging the Kinesthetic/Somatic Learners) and ask something like, "How many of you have experienced this topic as well?"
- "How many times have you ...?" When you want a factual answer.
- "Shout out the names of the places you've vacationed." Not a question, but a close-ended request for information.

You get the idea. The point is, you are not looking for dialogue at this time so the closed-ended question is a fantastic way to get people to engage, while not prolonging the conversation. It's an effective tool to use for your benefit as a Facilitator.

FACILITATION MYTH #9:
I MUST BE AN EXPERT AND HAVE ALL THE ANSWERS TO BE AN EFFECTIVE FACILITATOR.

TWO: *Use Your Space*

When you're "doing it," use your space. You may be prohibited by A/V (if the mic only works in a certain area), or room set, but if at all possible, use the room to your advantage.

When you walk the space, the audience in the room feels the shift in energy, especially when you come up close to them physically. It's important the entire group "feels" you at some point, not just the people in the front. (This action helps with Hecklers also and if you've only used the room to manage a Heckler, then it will be less impactful. How to deal with Hecklers is addressed in the next chapter.)

Also, if people have been sitting for a while, when you move around, they need to move and shift to keep up with you. It makes the body move and, as you already know, the mind and body are connected – if they're moving, they're learning.

THREE: *Using Improv Techniques*

In 1998, I took an improv class in NYC because, for seven minutes, I decided I was going to be a comedian. That statement was the funniest thing about me, by the way.

Clearly, my life didn't go in that direction, but the techniques I learned all those years ago have helped me immensely in my Facilitation life. Two of the most significant lessons I learned were:

- The **ART** of the "yes, and ..."
- Acknowledging your vulnerability

"Yes, and ..."

> Use your space and move around to engage your audience and connect the mind and body.

When you're on stage and your improv partner has established a scene where she is on Mars talking with E.T. and eating sushi, the worst thing you can do is to negate anything she has introduced. For example, if you say, "There's no Martian because I'm sitting on a horse in a Walgreens," it disassembles her work and set-up of the scene.

Whatever your scene partner suggests, you must acknowledge, validate and add to it. You could say, "Yes and I appreciate you ordering dinner, Honey. Be sure to keep the wasabi away from E.T.; he's highly allergic and only eats peanut butter." You've ensured the trust in your partner on stage, you've validated the data and the audience remains engaged.

What you've done here is to establish where you are, the situation, and the relationship between the two of you. You've shown respect to your partner and the emotional response will be reflected in their behavior on stage. This is exactly what happens when you use this technique in life.

When Facilitating, this technique is used often when a Participant answers a question wrong, as we discussed earlier. We may not like the scene that's been set for us on stage, but we can't negate it as we'll ruin, literally, the entire show. When we use the word BUT, what happens in general? The person to whom we're speaking is conditioned to not believe anything said prior to the BUT. While the word AND may just a fancy way around the BUT, your audience will continue to listen and trust as you've respected the authenticity of your Participant.

Acknowledging Your Vulnerability

Acknowledging your vulnerability is all about knowing that audiences can smell fear. When they smell it, they get anxious and tense. Our job as Facilitators of a message is to ensure we provide a safe environment for our audience to learn. Being tense is the opposite of where they should be.

During one improv show, there was a moment on stage where the audience was asked to create the scene and assign accents to the "comedians." I was assigned German. If you know me, you know that I think I can "do accents," but I really cannot and I absolutely panicked. As I went about the scene I knew my accent was terrible and I failed to use any of my learned improv skills; I could literally see the audience become uncomfortable. This made me more nervous, which led to the audience becoming even more uncomfortable.

When we got off the stage and I was sweating, a senior comedian pulled me aside and said, "You need to ease their pain and tell them the truth." "What?," I asked. Her point was, in moments where you're just lost, you need to look at the audience and say, "I have no idea what to say right now." Or, "does my German accent sound like a Russian accent to you?" Call yourself out. Do it with a smile and take complete unabashed ownership of it.

It was the most freeing advice I'd ever received. I use it like a champ to this day.

As a Facilitator, I often say to the audience, "Wait, what was I saying?" Or, "Stand by folks, I am not sure what's next." It doesn't matter – every single time I've acknowledged my vulnerability, my audience is completely forgiving. Never once have I heard a complaint, a judgment, or even a palpable heavy breath. I've done this on stage with 1,000 people and in meetings with CEOs. This is called being human and to humanize yourself to your audience only brings you more credibility.

> To humanize yourself to your audience only brings you more credibility.

FOUR: *Using A Whisper*

I love this technique. When I am making a specific point, one that is critical and has impact, I will crouch down and wave my hand so as to call everyone in, as if I'm telling them a secret. Wait for the Participants to physically respond by leaning in before you continue, then you know you've got their attention.

Then, in a whisper, tell them what you want to tell them. It always has an amazing effect, and I typically end it with, "You may want to write that down, but don't tell anyone."

Simple technique, but don't overuse it or then the emphasis on your chosen points will be lost. But, definitely work it in to help sell your most important topics/goals.

FIVE: *Using Your Body*

We've discussed using the room and your body. To reiterate, your body is an extended communicator and your audience is reading you physically even more than attaching the message to your words.

There's magic when you use your body to tell a story. I'm a tad gregarious so using my personal self comes easy for me. I narrate physically, naturally.

If you don't find this way of communicating natural, don't force it. Your audience will recognize your discomfort and respond negatively. Find the balance between what works for you and the space in which you find yourself. To do this, watch stand-up comedians and how they use their personalities and individual selves to utilize their surroundings to tell their story. Then, try some techniques on your own.

My absolute favorite way to use myself is when I'm transitioning from topic to topic. I'll narrate the fact that we're "moving on" and will walk from one side of the room to the other to showcase the physical message that is married to the verbal one. Sometimes you can do this with less space, by simply shifting your body from side to side.

The takeaway is, you have this beautiful canvas with which you can use to **ARTfully** narrate your message without words. Use it authentically and with purpose.

In Summary:

This chapter is where the **ART** of Facilitation really meets the science of Facilitation. The **ART** of communicating your message so it's remembered is delivered by engaging your audience, using your environment (which includes your body) and being authentically you. The irony about a chapter entitled "Actually Doing It" is that, you're NOT doing it; THEY are. Meaning, THEY are creating the data, THEY are learning and THEY are remembering. The more your Participants are engaged and validated, the more you can be sure YOU'RE DOING IT right.

FACILITATION MYTH #10:
TELLING IS TEACHING.

CHAPTER NINE
Handling Hecklers

Ridicule is the tribute paid to the genius by the mediocrities.
OSCAR WILDE

Here's why Hecklers can wreck you as a Facilitator – because you internalize and believe the heckle is about you personally. I'm here to tell you, it never is.

Hecklers are usually coming from a few different places:

- An overall feeling of inadequacy
- Boredom
- A desperate need to be validated
- Anger. Never at you – always from a someone or something that happened prior, or in general.

> Hecklers are ATTENTION SEEKERS; their behaviors are a result of their own 'noise.'

To really understand a Heckler, we need to go a little deep. Just a little.

A Heckler is an attention seeker. Attention seekers are most likely looking to be seen for a reason. Now, we'll never know the real/intimate reason (unless we get to know the Heckler), but here's what we do know – the heckle is coming from the "noise" inside the Heckler's head and it's driving them to be an interruption.

What is the noise you ask? Remember the chapter around the Fear Brain? We all have a voice or an inner critic that gets noisy sometimes. This "noise" can be intense and it can go deep, telling us something like the following:

- I'm scared …
- I'm not good enough …
- I'm too old to …
- I'm not prepared enough to …
- I'm not educated enough to …

I don't care what your "noise" is, but at some point in our lives, we've all heard the "noise" and given into the "noise." Maybe not in the behavior of a Heckler, but in other ways. An example of this could be thinking to yourself "I'm too old to go back to school" and then it was decided "Yes, I am too old. Everyone there will be young and I won't fit in and I won't be accepted. I'm not going."

The "noise" you hear is your little inner-you trying to keep you safe. You see, if you listen to the "noise" in the example above and don't go back to school, then you save yourself. You save yourself the potential embarrassment of being called out and not knowing an answer. Or, perhaps someone does "dis" you for being 20 years older and that will hurt. Well, if you don't even try, then you are saving yourself from embarrassment or pain.

You see, the "noise" is actually there to protect us because if we don't even try, then we can't fail.

> **SEE APPENDIX (p. 168)** for tips on handling hecklers.

However, sometimes it attempts to protect us in a way that actually has us act out or act up in ways that are socially unacceptable and, ironically, hurtful. Enter, the Heckler.

Bullies are Hecklers. We have all heard enough about bullies to know they never hurt someone because they want to; it's because they're giving into the "noise." Hecklers are the same.

Now that you know a Heckler's motivation to heckle is from their "noise," we can begin the process of changing our perspective of a Heckler. When we change our perspective and understand where the Heckler is coming from, we can empathize and begin to be understanding with a Participant who is acting up and heckling in class.

Here are possible ways to handle Hecklers:

1. **Know, it's Not YOU.** Remember to take a breath and know that the person who's getting in the way is hurting or scared and is doing the only thing they can to feel good or safe. Immediately ask yourself, "I wonder what's really going on for this person?"

2. **Vent When Necessary.** Allowing participants to vent can be productive, as long as it isn't allowed to escalate. Demonstrate active listening by making eye contact, nodding, paraphrasing, and confirming. Remember, you can acknowledge a Heckler without agreeing and this is a good time/place to do so. Senior Facilitators know when the lid is about to explode with their groups and if a venting session will help to get a person or group back on track. Don't be afraid of it, let the venting occur, but be mindful. Venting can turn to a complaint-session very quickly so know when it's time to let the venting be over and get back to the task at hand. I like to use the visualization "I have an empty jar in my hand" technique. I will say to the Heckler or to a group, "Do you see this empty jar in my hand? I'm taking the lid off and will ask you to fill it

with everything you need to get out; all your emotion and thoughts. Let's fill it. And, when I say it's time to put the lid on and get back to task, then it's time to get back to task. Because today we're going to talk about what we can control. But first, let's hear it ..." Then go about allowing the Heckler to vent, perhaps facilitate to any solutions and eventually put the lid back on the jar. It's a very good technique and ensures the group feels heard and respected without a massive derail of your event.

3. **Acknowledge and Diagnose.** When in front of a room of people, you must not allow the Heckler to sabotage your experience. Acknowledge the Heckler's feelings, but correct the reality by attempting to get to the root cause. Use questions, observations, and your gut to investigate the person's reality within the time limit provided. Demonstrate active listening and reassure the Heckler that you "get it." Then, get to a final resolve by putting the ball in their court with a choice of 2–3 options and, if necessary, a final question to get confirmation that it's okay to take up the topic later in the day. For example, "Gerry, can we agree to shelve this topic until the break and then we'll pick it back up again?"

4. **Sidebar.** If the Heckler persists, pull them aside during an activity or break and have a sidebar conversation. This is the time to acknowledge their behavior and simply ask, "Hey, what's going on for you?" This will allow a better chance for the Participant to open up and allow his/her reality to be shared, then you can work through it together. If the emotion or behavior is just too debilitating, you may need to ask them him/her to leave the experience altogether, and the conversation with the participant should absolutely be held in private.

5. **Stand and Touch.** Use your movement throughout the room to subtly address the Heckler. Stand near the Heckler that is having side conversations or are making

snide remarks to others. It's hard for a Heckler to heckle when you're literally standing on top of them. If the person doesn't stop, simply put your hand on their elbow. Most of the time, it will end by your mere presence alone.

In Summary:

Handling Hecklers is a challenge that you will eventually face. The key is to be ready with a few techniques, to remain calm in the face of perceived conflict and remember, it's not about you.

FACILITATION MYTH #11:
HECKLING IS ALL ABOUT ME.

CHAPTER TEN
Put a Bow on It

No great thing is created suddenly.
EPICTETUS

Ending a speech, or a class, or a keynote must be done with impact. With a call to action. As you've learned, you start your communication by telling them what you're going to tell them, then you tell them, then you end by telling them what you told them. Bookends only work if there are two.

As you start strong, you must end strong to give your people closure and ensure they know of the action they must take, the change they must make, or the thought you want them to have. They can do this via quiet reflections or enthusiastically; whatever way reinforces your message best.

After you've completed your last activity or shared the last point, the time has come for the bow. Some of my favorite ways to end are the most simple, yet have a ton of impact.

For example:

- A video – either one that's produced to make your point or one you've pulled from the internet with approval.

- A collage of images taken from the experience – this is very easy to do as there's so much technology

> Always acknowledge the close of your event by THANKING your Participants for their time and energy.

out there that can collect images from a cell phone and place them into a slide show. This is a super way to visually remind the Participants of all they experienced.

- Final team share – give everyone the chance to share with the group; it reinforces personal take-aways, bonds the group, and reminds others of topics they may have not thought to put on their own take-away list.

  SEE APPENDIX (p. 171) for suggestions on how to "put a bow on it."

- "Family Feud" competition. Split the group in two and have them answer questions learned throughout the experience Participant by Participant. Call a tie at the end or have small prizes ready for the winning team.

- Have the Participants write themselves a letter. Each Participant is handed paper and an envelope and asked to write a letter to his/her future self about who they will be after they apply their newly learned skills or information. They then put it into an envelope, seal it, and address it. (Preferably to their home; mail can tend to get lost when going to an office.) Hold onto the letters and send them a few months later. This guarantees that the personal take-away is captured and is my personal favorite "bow-tying" method.

However you decide to close out your experience, be sure to always be grateful for your Participant's time and energy. The last thing you must say before you bid your audience good-bye, turn the music up, and provide any significant final information, is to say thank you.

And then, with your **ARTful** support, off they go into the world with instruction on how to change it for the better.

In Summary:

Putting a bow on it is where you tell them what you told them; the latter half of your **ARTfully** facilitated bookend. The goal of the close of your presentation, keynote, course or even conversation is a call-to-action. Yes of course you want the end to be memorable and even uplifting; however ensure your people leave you reminded of the critical message for which they MUST remember and the ACTION for which they must take.

FACILITATION MYTH #12:
THE CLOSE IS ONLY ABOUT MOTIVATION.

STEP THREE

The ART of Building Your Brand

WHEN I STARTED BEING ME, I didn't realize that everything I said, everything I wore, every characteristic I displayed, and every syllable I accentuated would be judged and measured. As a result of another person's judgment and measurement, I would either be dismissed or followed.

Welcome to being a human BRAND.

No one told me when I was perfecting the **ART** of being ME that I was creating my own brand. In the beginning, no one told me there was such a thing as being "too funny," or "too entertaining" or "too fast." I learned these lessons all alone; the results of my actions and my branding choices resulted in being promoted or rehired or not.

Because no one told me, I want to be the one to give you the little gems of knowledge to ensure your future success. The key is that controlling what you can control is advice that does NOT stop during the **ART** of the Preparation phase.

If you want your brand to be seen the way you envision, you must:

- **ESTABLISH** yourself – create and become the "vision" of YOU. How do you want others to describe you as an **ARTful** Communicator?

- Be **CONSISTENT** – work on your brand everyday with total consistency.

Yes, my dear Reader, as a person who wants to be seen as an effective Communicator, be remembered, and gain repeat business you must establish your brand and apply techniques to create and sustain that brand. And control what you can, all the time.

CHAPTER ELEVEN
Establish Your ME

To establish yourself in the world a person must do all they can to appear already established.

FRANÇOIS DE LA ROCHEFOUCAULD

You've heard the phrase "fake it until you make it." Let me share a more impactful quote. "You become what you think about all day long."

Earl Nightingale communicated that message in the 1950's when teaching his sales team how to be successful. If you believe you're a success, you're a success. If you believe you can, you can.

Conversely, if you believe yourself to be poor at communicating, inarticulate, not humorous, etc., then you better believe, you are. The first step to creating your brand is believing in your brand; and, in this case, it means believing in you.

If you've read this far, you want to be the best, most **ARTful** Communicator ever born. Great, don't stop there – now believe that you can be. Easy, right? Well, of course not. I've worked on the **ART** of self-acceptance my whole life and honestly, the content of what I've learned and what I want to share lies within an entirely different book.

> Believe that you are the best Facilitator – and you WILL become the best.

I say I became the "best" Facilitator in the world the day I believed I was. Today, I feel so happy and confident within my brand and I share that brand every time I communicate.

That last bit sounded pretty conceited didn't it? The truth is, I may not be the best Communicator in the world, but I am the best ME in the world.

The conversation or debate is not around whether or not I nor anyone else is the best, the conversation is around the fact that my brand is MINE. I created it and it's universally mine. When I say I'm the "best," it's not meant to be cocky – it means that I am truly the best at being the ME that I've created.

You know where I'm the worst? Being YOU. Or, being Simon Sinek, or Oprah, or Chelsea Handler. I can never communicate like them and that's great, because THEY are the best at being THEM.

And, YOU are the BEST at being YOU.

Can you take characteristics you like and emulate others? YES. A lot of my brand was borrowed; some say the sincerest form of flattery is imitation. I flat out borrowed! To be clear, when I say "borrowed," I really mean I observed, learned, and adapted. We can't just copy another Facilitator and think we'll be the best. We need to watch, observe, attempt, and make the technique work for ourselves. You must watch the pros and personalize, never just copy and paste.

I learned so much from Ron Chatwin and Nancy Korte, my first and best mentors in the business. To this day, I pay a silent homage to them when I'm "doing my thing."

It's great to borrow, but not OK to copy. Be authentic, be YOU.

It's time to begin the journey of creating your character and believe in it. How to start? Here's the space where you use the **ARTful** techniques from this book to really visualize the YOU that you want to be. First, answer these questions honestly:

- How much energy do I always bring?
- What type of Learner am I and how must I adapt?
- How will I use my nerves to my advantage?
- What does my environment always look like and have; even when I can't completely control my space?
- What type of clothes am I wearing? (Unless of course a client dictates.)
- What are my brand colors?
- How am I wearing my hair, makeup, do I have a signature piece of clothing like socks, pocket square, etc.?
- What's my signature opening? Closing?
- What is my primary communication strength? How can I use it?
- How will I use my body to tell the story?
- What can I giveaway?
- What else about YOU can you bring to each and every communication?

After answering these questions honestly, from the heart, they will paint a picture of who you are and help you figure out on what you need to work. For example, you've read earlier about my acknowledgment that I talk fast, and I continue to work on this trait. As I want to be seen as an effective Communicator, I consciously talk slower even when in situations where it's not critical so as to practice and continue to improve my brand.

Once you've done your homework and know the characteristics you want to have, the goals you want to achieve, and the humor/style/actions, etc. you want to use, now you can start to use them.

We've already learned that the brain is a funny thing. While we can't control anyone else in this great world of ours, there is one thing that is in our total control – our thoughts.

You already learned all about visualization techniques. Picture yourself actually using these techniques while delivering that keynote, or that presentation to the board, or the conflict conversation you have to have with your boss. Picture yourself actually saying the words, picture the audience reacting, nay, responding around you. Acknowledge how you feel. Then do it again, and again, and again.

I had already been a professional speaker for many, many years, yet I was not confident just prior to a recent presentation to an executive board, even though I knew the material by heart.
I had lost sight of the ME I knew I was because I was very concerned about this audience and their judgment, etc. As a result, I was losing my authentic ME, started to doubt my ME, and my ME was in panic mode.

Luckily, I knew what to do. First, remember my ME. Who is Tina and who is the ME that must show up? To be authentic and ME. The only ME on the planet! I had already visualized the ME presenting for weeks leading up to the event. I was owning my characteristics, my style, my room set, my risk-taking humor, etc. I did that until I couldn't even imagine not showing up as ME. And, I practiced being ME.

Minutes before presenting, I was quite nervous. However, I wasn't debilitated. I acknowledged the moment, breathed, continued to visualize up until seconds before, and then lived my ME on stage. Was it perfect? No. Did the audience know? No. Was it a success? Yeah, it was.

Recognize that when we put energy into being the person we think we should be, or the client, or the boss wants us to be, we stop being ourselves and you stop being the BEST YOU. You'd be surprised how much energy we put into being the person we think others want us to be. Or, to communicate in the way we think other's want us to communicate. Stop. Stop that now.

In Summary:

Decide on your ME, define your ME, and then go be your ME.

Now that you've done your exercise and have the vision of the ME you want to be, it's time to live that ME everyday.

FACILITATION MYTH #13:
I'M TOO OLD TO CHANGE.

CHAPTER TWELVE
Maintain Your ME

*Integrity is doing the right thing,
even when no one is watching.*

C.S. LEWIS

I knew I "had arrived" as a brand when someone walked into my room by accident one day and said, "Oh, wrong room, this is clearly Tina's class. You all are in for a treat!"

Yes. Victory.

Showing up and bringing all of you, every time, to every experience, even if you're affecting only one person, is how you'll separate yourself from the pack. Having integrity by always knowing you're consistently respecting the **ART of Facilitation** will be your game changer.

We spoke about the characteristics of your brand, and using visuals as signage and how important they are. We learned the importance of kinesthetic devices on the table, and how to facilitate using questions. What we haven't talked about is when to do all of these things.

When?

The answer: ALL THE TIME.

By showing up using all of these skills and tools all the time, you're creating your consistent brand. You are establishing your ME. And this is what makes you **ARTful** and competitive. People will know what to expect, find comfort, and want you back. And you control all of it.

Being consistent does three things:

- **Establishes your reputation – and in this case, your brand.** Your business growth requires a track record of success. You can't establish a track record if you are constantly shifting gears or trying new tactics. Many efforts fail before they get to the finish line, but not because the tactic was flawed or goals weren't clear, it's because you simply didn't stay the course and keep providing the elevated **ARTful** Facilitation you know is critical to success.

> To be competitive and remembered, create your brand and live your brand CONSISTENTLY.

- **Separates you from the pack and makes you relevant.** Your employees and your customers need a predictable flow of information from you. So frequently Facilitators or even companies adopt an initiative or style and abandon some or all of it before it gains traction. Attach your brand to the tools and characterizes you use all the time.

- **Maintains your message and brand.** Your audience pays as much or more attention to what you do and your attention to detail as to what you say. Consistency in your Facilitation (which includes all the choices you make before and after your experience) serves as a model for how others form their own standards and even, behave. If you treat a meeting as unimportant, don't be surprised when others around you (customers, employees, potential sales clients, etc.) decrease their level of care and interest and possibly, even leave you.

Marketers will tell us that as consumers, when we buy, we typically buy what we've bought before. In other words, we make purchases based on the comfort of knowing the level of quality we've purchased in the past and will trust that we will receive that same level of quality again. What's really interesting here is, the product we purchase may not be the best, but we don't care because the comfort of trusting the level of quality we'll receive trumps the fear of trying something new and experiencing failure.

That my friends, is called branding. And that is how you create a competitive environment for yourself; show up as you with consistency and you'll be invited back to the show.

Back to how you feel. We spoke about the brain and how we can control everything we can control to reduce stress and tension in our Participants. By always producing sameness, believe it or not you've done two things – created familiarity which provides a subtle tension reduction and, created a competitive environment where your Participants will remember your brand consistently; and customers want consistency.

In Summary:

By being consistent in your delivery you can effectively create a loyal customer base with your Participants. You will build a subconscious confidence in your products and services resulting in your customer's trust that they'll have a **consistent** experience each and every time. Magic.

FACILITATION MYTH #14:
CUSTOMERS ARE LOYAL
TO A QUALITY PRODUCT ALONE.

CONCLUSION

When I buy a new book, I always read the last page first, that way in case I die before I finish, I know how it ends.

NORA EPHRON, *WHEN HARRY MET SALLY*

WRITING THIS BOOK WAS A LABOR OF LOVE. I love the **ART of Facilitation** and the only thing I enjoy more than writing about facilitating, is facilitating about facilitating.

As discussed, so many of the techniques and ideas presented here can be used in life, and have personally helped me to elevate and grow as a better person, not just a better Facilitator. I have absolute confidence that when applying some of your new found skills, you too will reap the benefits that I have.

As this book was dedicated to my dear friend, mentor and **ARTful Facilitator**, Ron Chatwin, I leave you with perhaps my favorite piece of advice from him. You heard me throughout the book reference *control what you can control*. Ron would say this with even more eloquence: "If you can predict it, you can prepare for it." He taught me this years ago and the advice has prepared me for success time and time again.

You now have the tools to prepare for whatever can and will happen during the course of your experience as you have the knowledge to predict the potential left turns you will undoubtedly encounter. Take his words to heart, use the tools and you'll for sure, be unstoppable.

To regale me with your successes or to answer any question you have, I'd love to hear from you via tina.clements@rpc-partners.com. Until then my friend, be **ARTful**, and have fun changing the world!

Enjoy the **ART** my friends – go forth and change lives; starting with your own!

FACILITATION MYTH #15:
ONE PERSON CAN'T CHANGE THE WORLD.

APPENDICES
Handout Templates

THE ART OF FACILITATION
PREWORK TOOLBOX

COMMUNICATION CHECKLIST:

- ☐ Where is the event?
  - ☐ Address
  - ☐ Meeting room
  - ☐ Directions from lobby/entrance
- ☐ Where should they park?
- ☐ Who handles transportation?
- ☐ What time should they arrive?
- ☐ When does the event start? Is breakfast/meal provided earlier than start time?
- ☐ What's the dress code?
- ☐ Who handles meals?
  - ☐ Breakfast
  - ☐ Lunch
  - ☐ Dinner
- ☐ What's the schedule? (High-level is ok)
- ☐ What should they bring?
- ☐ Is there pre-work?
- ☐ Who is the contact if they have questions?
  - ☐ Travel
  - ☐ Course content

THE ART OF FACILITATION
PREWORK TOOLBOX

ROOM SETUP CHECKLIST:

Signage:
- ☐ Lobby/Entrance to your Room
- ☐ Supports corporate identity

Music:
- ☐ Entrance: High energy, not too loud, zero profanity
- ☐ Activity: Lower volume, slower pace, no words

Tables and Chairs:
- ☐ First choice: Table rounds with 6 or fewer chairs
- ☐ Second choice: U-shape

On the Tables:
- ☐ Pipe cleaners
- ☐ Play-Doh
- ☐ Koosh balls and Slinkys

Décor:
- ☐ Supports learning
- ☐ Relevant to the topic and themes
- ☐ Non-obvious

Scent:
- ☐ Scent is directly aligned with memory
- ☐ Keep it light—not overpowering
- ☐ Preferred: vanilla, cinnamon, and chocolate

THE ART OF FACILITATION
PREWORK TOOLBOX

BODY LANGUAGE CHECKLIST:

Communication is:
- 7% words
- 55% body language
- 38% voice and tone

People look for **congruency** among the words you say, your tone of voice, and your body language.

Body Language Self-Evaluation:

Eye Contact:
_____
_____

Posture:
_____
_____

Smile:
_____
_____

Stance:
_____
_____

Two things to improve:
_____
_____

THE ART OF FACILITATION
GESTURES AROUND THE WORLD

THE OFFENSIVE GESTURES MATCHING GAME:

GESTURE		MEANING
👍	Thumbs up	Sit on it. Australia, Greece, Middle East
✌️	Peace sign (palm facing in)	Up yours. We're excellent at archery. Australia, United Kingtom, South Africa
🖐️	Talk to the hand	I've had enough. Greece, Mexico, Africa, Middle East
👌	A-OK	A-hole. Greece, Spain, Brazil
🤘	Rock on!	Your wife is sleeping with someone else. Spain, Italy, Greece
👈	Come hither	You are a dog (and come here). Philippines, Slovakia, East Asia, Singapore
🤞	Good luck!	Lady parts. Vietnam
👉	Pointing	Used to indicate an inanimate object. China, Japan, Indonesia, Latin America

# THE ART OF FACILITATION TOOLBOX

FILLER FUNNIES, WHISKER WORDS, AND SILENCE:

Filler Funnies:
- Bad jokes
- Attempts to fill the silence
- Happens fast, and happens because of nerves
- Examples: "Is this mic on?" "Tough audience!"

Whisker Words:
- Random words or phrases
- Used to buy time to think
- Examples:
  - ☐ Um
  - ☐ You Know
  - ☐ Ah
  - ☐ In other words
  - ☐ So
  - ☐ At the end of the day

Silence:
1. When is silence ok?

2. When is silence NOT ok?

3. What's the solution?

My favorite whisker word or filler funny (that I'm going to stop using):

THE ART OF FACILITATION TOOLBOX

HANDLING NERVES – **BEFORE** THE EVENT

Know your audience:
- Who will you be teaching?
- How can you connect with them?
- Which emotions will they respond to?
- What will they get out of it?

Know your material:
- Active reading = pen or highlighter in hand
- Make an outline
- Throw the book away!
- Study and prep from your outline

Practice:
- Practice each module
- Don't cram—spend a little time each day
- Avoid overloading your brain

Prepare:
- Handle the logistics
- Email or communicate with your participants
- Pack your bag
- Plan your arrival and first evening: transportation, meetings, meals

Two things you will try:
_____
_____

THE ART OF FACILITATION TOOLBOX

HANDLING NERVES – **DURING** THE EVENT

Breathing:
- Remember to breathe!
- Your brain needs oxygen to function
- Controlling breathing helps control nerves

Hydrate:
- Drink plenty of water
- Have water on-hand throughout the day

Slow Down:
- Conversations are fast
- Teaching is slow
- Use pauses to punctuate

Smile:
- Your body influences how you feel
- Smiling makes you happier
- Smiling conveys confidence

Remember: It's about them!
- They don't care as much about you as you do
- Focus your energy on the audience and you'll forget about yourself

Two things you will try:
_____
_____

THE ART OF FACILITATION
TOOLBOX

HANDLING HECKLERS:

Diagnose the issue:
- Ask questions to determine the root cause of the issue
- Can be done in the moment or during a break

Acknowledge and validate:
- Acknowledge the feelings but correct the reality
- Reassure the heckler that you "get it"
- Put the ball in their court: offer 2-3 options

Vent when necessary
- Venting releases energy
- Venting can be productive if it isn't allowed to escalate

Stand and Touch:
- Use movement to subtly address the heckler
- Stand near hecklers that are holding side conversations
- Touch on the shoulder

Sidebar:
- If the heckler persists, pull them aside during an activity or break
- Ask how you can resolve the issue and offer options

REMEMBER! Heckling isn't about you.

Notes:
_____
_____

THE ART OF FACILITATION TOOLBOX

POWERPOINT:

PowerPoint is a compliment to your content.

Making PowerPoint:
- ☐ Use fewer words, more images (example: our housekeeping slide)
- ☐ Aim for six bullets per slide, six words per bullet
- ☐ Keep the font size BIG
- ☐ Use common, easy-to-read fonts: Helvetica, Verdana, Arial
- ☐ Keep content out of the corners
- ☐ Stick with the company's Corporate Identity (CI) guidelines

Presenting with PowerPoint:
- ☐ Don't compete with your slides
- ☐ Don't read the slides or describe the pictures—they should be self-explanatory
- ☐ Manage your audience's attention. Buy a clicker with a blank screen button
- ☐ Embed videos or audio for a seamless, fluid presentation
- ☐ Use PowerPoint as your cheat sheet

Notes:
_____
_____

THE ART OF FACILITATION TOOLBOX

TECHNOLOGY SUCCESS TIPS

Prepare:
- Get a list of everything you need before the event
- Think about charging, projecting, and distributing technology
- How will you make your audience comfortable with the technology?

Setup:
- Go to the venue ahead of time
- Set up and test your technology
- Test Wi-Fi strength
- Identify issues before the event, when you can still fix them

Practice:
- People won't use technology if they find it difficult or complex
- Practice your technology introduction and explanations
- Make it easy for them

Access to an expert:
- Who can you call when a problem occurs?

Notes:
_____
_____

THE ART OF FACILITATION TOOLBOX

PUTTING A BOW ON IT:

Why we do it? Attention AND Retention
- Emotions get our attention
- We process meaning before details
- We can't multitask – control their takeaway
- Tell them what you told them
- Call to action

Some Examples:

Ball Toss

This is a simple activity where you get participants out of their seats and toss a ball around the circle. Each person shares a takeaway, then tosses the ball to the next participant.

Review Quiz

This game requires some preparation, but can be high-energy, fun, and competitive. You divide participants into teams and they take turns answering questions and earning points. The team with the most points gets a prize at the end.

Postcard to Future Self

This is an individual reflection activity where participants write a postcard or note that you will send 1-2 months after the training. They write down all of the things learned in the training and 1-2 things they hope they've implemented. This is also an inexpensive and low-effort form of post-event follow-up.

Steps and Leaps

This is an informal way to create an action plan, starting with a big goal (leap), then defining the key milestones (steps), and ending with a small action that can be taken immediately.

Thank You Notes

This activity boosts the group dynamic. Each person writes a thank you note to someone else in the meeting, citing a specific contribution the other person brought to the group.

THE ART OF FACILITATION TOOLBOX

ACTIVITY DESIGN BASICS:

STEP 1: Preparation
- Music, aromas, visuals
- Positive suggestions
- Clear, meaningful goals
- Learner benefits (WIIFM?)
- Pre-course learner prep kit
- Positive social environment
- Total learner involvement
- Curiosity arousal

STEP 2: Presentation
Passive
Initial encounter with the material
Facilitator leads, learners do

Three steps:
1. Facilitator presentation
   - Use props and visuals
   - Tell a story with human interest
   - Process course—use the wall
2. Facilitator/Learner presentations
   - Write an exam and test your partner
   - Group discussions
3. Learner presentations and discovery exercises
   - Team presentation
   - Model building
   - Field trip

STEP 3: Practice
- Active!
- Heart of Accelerated Learning—goal is 70%
- Team brainstorm and presentations
- Creating a process
- Creating tools

STEP 4: Performance
- Goal = Ensure that the learning sticks and is applied
- At the session:
  - Evaluation (tests, orals, etc.)
  - Evaluate and enhance the learning
  - Action planning and next steps
- After the session:
  - Reinforcement (mentoring and support groups)
  - Organizational support
  - Post-event on-the-job evaluations

Notes:

THE ART OF FACILITATION
TOOLBOX

TYPES OF ACTIVITIES:

Individual reflection:
- Useful as a pause in the activities (Let the participant think and rest)
- Recap main learning points
- Let the student pick 1-2 things to apply

Team discussion and feedback:
- Access the knowledge in the room
- Facilitate a discussion—guide, but don't present
- Validate the group's knowledge, experience, and ideas

Team activity, presentation to the group, and feedback:
- Students create their own process, tools, or solutions
- Teams present to the group and receive feedback

Team practice activity and debrief:
- Students work in pairs or triads to practice a concept
- Students give and receive feedback within their groups
- Facilitator conducts overall debrief after each round

Plenary (group) activity
- Activities with the large group
- 1-2 students volunteer, the group observes and offers feedback
  - Evaluation (tests, orals, etc.)

Notes:
_____
_____

BUSTED: 15 MYTHS THAT HOLD YOU BACK

FACILITATION MYTH #1:
IT'S ALL ABOUT ME.

FACILITATION MYTH #2:
EVERYONE LEARNS THE SAME WAY.

FACILITATION MYTH #3:
YOU HAVE NO CONTROL OVER YOUR PARTICIPANTS' FEELINGS.

FACILITATION MYTH #4:
THAT'S NOT MY JOB.

FACILITATION MYTH #5:
A SLIDE DECK MUST CONTAIN ALL THE DATA.

FACILITATION MYTH #6:
TECHNOLOGY ALWAYS ADDS VALUE.

FACILITATION MYTH #7:
SUCCESSFUL COMMUNICATION IS ALL ABOUT WHAT YOU SAY.

FACILITATION MYTH #8:
PROS DON'T GET NERVOUS.

FACILITATION MYTH #9:
I MUST BE AN EXPERT
AND HAVE ALL THE ANSWERS
TO BE AN EFFECTIVE FACILITATOR.

FACILITATION MYTH #10:
TELLING IS TEACHING.

FACILITATION MYTH #11:
HECKLING IS ALL ABOUT ME.

FACILITATION MYTH #12:
THE CLOSE IS ONLY
ABOUT MOTIVATION.

FACILITATION MYTH #13:
I'M TOO OLD TO CHANGE.

FACILITATION MYTH #14:
CUSTOMERS ARE LOYAL
TO A QUALITY PRODUCT ALONE.

FACILITATION MYTH #15:
ONE PERSON CAN'T CHANGE
THE WORLD.

RECOGNITION

A very special thank you to those who have taught me the **ART**, have respected the **ART** and encouraged me to share the **ART** over the years. To the rpc team who adopted **ARTful** Facilitation into their daily lives and brings me joy every day. To Christian Feilmeier who always says yes. To my brother and sister Facilitators and Developers from whom I continue to learn and borrow. To Dave Sweet who said first, "Hey kid, you're good." To Nancy Korte, who taught me the **ART** of the ah-ha and how to be authentically me no matter what. To my brilliant Mom, who said, "You should major in Communications." To my family who loves me and finally, to Ron Chatwin, whose integrity and kindness of heart makes him my scarecrow – thanks for always modeling the person I want to be when I grow up.

HIRE TINA TO SPEAK OR FACILITATE

Make a real impact at your next event or workshop with Tina as your keynote speaker or workshop facilitator. In her keynote "Yes, You Do Have a Choice," Tina delivers an empowering message on how to maximize your potential through the power of choice. Through personal and engaging storytelling, she reveals how living in the blame-game blocks productivity and detracts from individual and organizational success. If you're looking to elevate your audience's decision-making ability, this keynote is the perfect way to jumpstart an overall mind-shift and culture change.

Tina's workshop aptly named "The ART of Facilitation" has inspired hundreds of people who have become facilitation warriors. Her vibrant, funny, and energetic style ignites all audiences, whether they're independent participants, departments, or entire companies. Tina can bring her workshop to you or can deliver your own, personalized content. A highly sought-after professional speaker, Tina has consulted on a wide range of topics including employee engagement, leadership, giving feedback, talent management, customer experience, and Learning & Development. To learn more about hiring Tina, please visit www.rpcamerica.com.

ABOUT rpc

As consumers have more information at their fingertips and are less brand loyal, retail companies must find ways to create value and delight customers. rpc is a consulting firm dedicated to helping you create a culture of high performers and ways to connect with your customer base in more engaging and meaningful ways. After a comprehensive assessment, we partner with you to find the ideal solution to the challenges you face. Whether it's training and motivating employees, recruiting top talent, coaching teams to reach their maximum potential, or data analysis to elevate your customers' experience, our proven methodology and product line will take your business to the next level of success.

ABOUT TINA

Tina Clements is a high energy, hands-on keynote speaker, author, coach, facilitator, and successful leader. Before launching the BMW Group Joint Venture, The Retail Performance Company, LLC (rpc) in 2013, she worked for 10+ years within the BMW NA Organization and has been in the Learning & Development industry since 1996. Throughout her career, she has held leadership positions such as Vice President, Operations Manager, and Training Manager. Believing that a company's success is directly related to the engagement of its people, she excels at moving businesses forward and motivating and growing talent. Tina has worked with organizations such as HBO, Volkswagen, MINI, IBM, WVIP Radio/Cable Systems, and boutique firms such as automätik education. Always challenging herself to improve and grow, she has earned CPC and ELI-MP accreditations among others, such as: DiSC®, MBTI®, and Langevin©.

BOOK CLUB QUESTIONS

1) What message stood out for you the most and why?

2) What feelings did this book evoke for you?

3) If you got the chance to ask the author one question, what would it be?

4) What do you think the author's purpose was in writing this book? What ideas was she trying to get across?

5) Based on your previous knowledge of the subject, what was something new you took away from this book?

6) How will you apply new concepts you've learned into your own practice?

7) Based on the tone of the book, what do you think Tina is like in person?

8) If you were making a movie of this book, who would you cast?

CPSIA information can be obtained
at www.ICGtesting.com
Printed in the USA
LVHW081256050121
675777LV00015B/90/J